The

Puppy Nanny's Guide
to
Training Your Puppy

Jude LeMoine

The Puppy Nanny's Guide to Training Your Puppy

Published by CreateSpace: Charleston, South Carolina, USA

Design & Production: Wendy Crumpler, wendycrumpler.com

ISBN 1-4701-9622-0

For all the dogs I've ever loved...

Major
Watson
Kurt
Gus
Spencer
Jack

The best of companions and
the most excellent of teachers

TABLE OF CONTENTS

The

Puppy Nanny's Guide

PUPPY IS COMING

. . . .

So, there's a puppy coming to your house!

Wow! That's exciting...but bit scary, too, if you think about it. This brand new creature will be totally dependent on you for the next 10-12 years. It will learn whatever you teach it.

Training never stops.

Puppies come from lots of places. Maybe your neighbour's dog has had pups and your whole family has fallen in love, or the breeder of your chosen breed has called to say, "Come see the puppies!" (I know that you're wise enough not to buy from a pet store.)... or your local shelter has puppies and you're all going for a visit.

If you're considering adopting an adult dog from a shelter, **please, please, please** do your research and be ready to work with this dog. Remember, well-mannered dogs aren't usually the ones that end up in shelters.

KNOW THIS:

Until the moment the puppy is in your car or in your house, you can still change your mind. Now's the time.

Are you still thinking it's a good idea?

Bringing home a puppy is a huge deal...in fact, it's a lifetime commitment. The first 8-10 weeks he is with you will require a huge slice of time and energy from your life not to mention money... the expenses of setting up for your new canine family member and the required vet visits will make a considerable dent in your wallet. The headiness of falling in love soon gives way to the trivial chores of every day. They make puppies cute for a reason, you know.

So...what then? Think I'm trying to talk you out of getting a puppy? Not a bit.

The time you spend training and playing with your puppy over the next few weeks will ensure a well-mannered family companion who will bring oodles of joy to you for the next 10-15 years (and even more, if you're lucky).

BE VERY SURE YOU ARE READY FOR THIS.

You still have time to change your mind.

HE'S HERE...THE EARLY DAYS

· ·

I sincerely hope you're reading this while you're in **"Maybe we'll get a puppy!"** mode. Having a plan will make Bozo's moving in much, much easier.

Even as I try to think of all that needs to happen in order for you to:

1. be ready to bring your puppy home, and;

2. integrate him into your family,

I feel the pressure of **"So much to do, so little time!"**

I have no gender bias regarding dogs. I have always owned male dogs and, therefore, my default setting is "he." Our puppy on these pages is, from now on, Bozo!

KNOW THIS:

It doesn't matter where you get your puppy (although I urge you NOT to buy from a pet store...I, for one, would like to see puppy mills disappear!). It doesn't matter what kind of puppy you get—big, small, purebred or mixed breed—they are all trainable.

Remember when you were in school? Didn't doing your homework make the exam much easier? The same is true here.

"What's puppy homework?" you ask.

Let's take it step by step.

1. Discuss, decide, agree within your family:

   🐾 **what** kind of puppy is coming?

   🐾 **when** is puppy coming?

   🐾 **who** will be principally responsible?

   A puppy is a *family affair*. Mom (or whoever the principal caregiver is to be) doesn't have to do it *all*, but she does have to make sure it gets *done*.

2. Talk to vets, trainers, breeders, and puppy owners (whenever and wherever you meet them). This is your research! Read books, watch videos, surf the net (www.dogstardaily.com is one of my favourite *'go-to's'*). Listen to everyone, take all they have to offer, but make your *own* decisions. As with raising children, common sense in puppy care and training goes a long way.

3. Shop.

   Before you bring Bozo home, you will need to buy:

   🐾 A crate. You will also need washable bedding. There will be accidents.

   🐾 A leather or woven nylon leash. While a retractable leash might be great for for a leash-trained dog, it does not work for training.

- 🐾 A flat closure (i.e. buckle) nylon or leather collar. Buy inexpensive. You'll be sizing up several times over the next few months.

- 🐾 A water bowl. You can use any unbreakable, stable bowl you already have.

- 🐾 5 or 6 stuffable toys[1]. Kongs® (www.kongcompany.com) are virtually indestructible and therefore a good choice. Premier Pet Toys (www.premier.com) makes quality products as well. These may appear to be big-ticket items, but I can assure you that they are well worth the money! Hollow bones are also good…just be sure that you buy the length appropriate for your puppy.

- 🐾 Good quality kibble. Read the label. Personally, I look for meat as the #1 ingredient and I don't want to see 'corn' at all.

- 🐾 Liver treats. I tell you how to make your own at the end of this book. Cheap and easy!

- 🐾 A baby gate or exercise pen (depending on where you will confine your puppy for long periods). A bathroom or laundry room makes a great area for this. Be sure to puppy proof! You'd be amazed at what curious, curious creatures these puppies are! Remove the toilet paper from its holder, elevate wastebaskets, towels, detergents, etc. You're older and wiser. Think like a puppy.

---

[1] Stuffable toys are rubber chew toys into which you can put kibble and other treats.

Are you ready?

I see young and old dogs every day here at The Dog House (our dog daycare & boarding facility). I also see lots of unacceptable behaviours...dogs shy of people, wary of new places, anxious about meeting new dogs, guarding the ball or their food, occasional bites (some causing harm) and house soiling (this seems to be a behaviour seen mostly in small dogs).

ALL of these unwanted behaviours can be avoided *IF* (and it's a big *IF* and an even bigger commitment) new owners follow the important early development guidelines.

"Huh?"

Imagine a wide-open window. Gradually, it begins to slide until it closes.

Puppy at birth = wide-open window

Puppy at 16 weeks = window closed

Yes, you can teach Bozo after 16 weeks and, of course, you will! What's below is simply best and easiest taught while the window is wide open.

Early Development Guidelines

1. Establish house rules and a chew toy hobby

2. Socialize your puppy to people (and lots of them!)

3. Teach your puppy bite inhibition

4. Socialize your puppy to other dogs/puppies

PUPPIES PEE. PUPPIES POOP.

· ·

Not surprising at all, when you think about it. What goes in must come out. The problem arises when they eliminate in *your* house, on *your* rug (and countless other inappropriate places). This is where *you* come in. It is absolutely 100% up to you to manage where your puppy's toilet is and to see that he uses it.

Even one accident in the house, while only a tiny puddle or pile, is *bad news*. It will inevitably lead to more. If Bozo has an accident, roll up a newspaper and smack yourself sharply on the head while asking, "What did I *not* do?" Bozo is simply being a normal puppy. Got that?

Let's get this right from the very beginning.

You and Bozo are in the car heading for home. He's just left his birth family for the first time. You pull into the driveway or garage. If Bozo has his collar on, great! Attach the leash, put him on the ground and move quickly and enticingly saying, "Bozo, come!" in a high pitched tone while moving backwards (don't trip!) or at least sideways, towards your goal: his previously determined toilet area. You will find 'lure treats' to be very helpful in this endeavour, so go ahead and use them. It's his kibble, remember?

If it's a long distance to the toilet from the car, carry Bozo part way but be sure to let him get there, at least partway, on his own. (The jiggling helps move what needs to come out!) When you reach your goal, stand still and let him circle around you as he most likely will. Wait three minutes...you may need a timer for this...it will seem a long time to you. When Bozo has *finished* peeing and/or pooping, be lavish with praise and treats.

- Say: "Yes!" Give treat. Say: "Yes!" Give treat. Say" "Yes!" Give treat. Say: "What a good dog! What a clever boy!" And so on. This is a big deal and it's important for you to let Bozo know he has done a good thing.

- Move away from the toilet area. Let him explore for a few minutes.

If Bozo doesn't perform, it's no big deal. He will. For now, it's time to take Bozo into the house and **straight into his long-term confinement area.**

"But the entire family can't fit into the laundry room and we all want to hang out with our new puppy."

Well, for now, you'll have to hang out with him one or two at a time. You must keep in mind that potty training at this stage is absolutely crucial.

Set your timer for the top of the hour and take Bozo again to his outdoor toilet area. Praise and treat him for his performance. Return to confinement area if nothing happens after three to four minutes. Reset your time for the top of the hour. Why every hour? Do puppies pee/poop every hour on the hour? No, of course not. The whole idea of the timer is to prevent accidents and enable you to predict when Bozo does need to go. Bear in mind that animals do not choose to soil their sleeping areas. It's only fair, then, to set Bozo up for success by keeping the close confinement (crate) time to one-hour stretches.

While on the subject of toilets, let's talk about setting up a toilet area in Bozo's long-term confinement area. Depending on whether you live in a rural or urban setting, the materials required for this are slightly different but the concept remains the same.

Rural Setting

Materials:

- A kitty litter pan or similar shallow low-sided container

- A piece of sod cut to fit the bottom of the pan. You will likely want to purchase a roll of sod (available at any garden centre), as it will eventually need to be changed.

Method:

- Clean up poop just as you would outside. Change the sod when your nose tells you to. Keep in mind that the smell of urine will be important to Bozo's success, so don't be too fastidious!

Urban Setting

Materials:

- A kitty litter pan or similar shallow low-sided container

- Kitty litter

🐕 A couple of ceramic floor tiles turned rough side up. The tiles should cover, as completely as possible, the bottom of the pan.

Method:

🐕 Put kitty litter in pan. Place tiles on top of litter. (This approximates the concrete/asphalt surfaces of the city dweller.) Clean up poop just as you would outside. Change the kitty litter frequently.

Exploring his entire new home is **not** an option for Bozo at this point. That's a privilege he **earns** one room at a time as his potty training progresses. Do not cave in to the pleas of your children or grandchildren. They will have lots of time with Bozo in the not-too-distant future! Sure, Bozo can be in the kitchen, living room, dining area or wherever else you want him but unless someone is closely supervising him, he should be in his crate happily chewing a stuffed chewtoy.

BOZO'S SAFE PLACE...THE CRATE

If you've done your homework well (and I've every reason to believe you have...after all, you're reading this book!) and chosen a breeder who home-raises puppies, chances are good that Bozo will already be familiar with 'the crate.'

Many dogs will seek out a cave-like space under a desk or behind a chair next to a wall so I know the 'cave' concept is agreeable to them. The crate is Bozo's moveable haven. It needs to be big enough for him to move and turn around in, but not so big that he'll want to use it as his own private toilet. The crate will need a washable pad or cushion in it and you'll want to have it near you most of the time when you're at home—in the kitchen, TV room, home office, or even bedroom... wherever you tend to spend the most time.

You, too, need to think of the crate as a haven, a safe space for Bozo. I used to think of crates as unpleasant confinement. Not so. When I got Gus as a nine-week-old puppy (long before I knew what I know now) I had **none** of the necessary skills required to crate train him. His barking, screaming, and general hootin' and hollerin' won. He was **never** crate trained and it took me **nine months** to teach him where the appropriate toilet was!

Smack in the head, Jude! What did I do wrong? EVERYTHING.

So let's crate train YOUR puppy from the start... beginning on the day you bring him home.

If Bozo's never seen a crate before, put one in his long-term confinement area on opposite side of the space from his indoor toilet. Keep the door propped open and let him take his time to check it out. A couple of pieces of kibble strategically placed inside will definitely increase his desire to investigate!

KNOW THIS:

Training is best done when Bozo is hungry (i.e. just before breakfast, lunch, dinner, and his evening feeding). And just so you know? Bozo will need four meals a day until he's 12-14 weeks old.

Did we talk about measuring Bozo's daily ration of kibble into a small bag or container each day? This is important. This is your working/training ration for the day. We're **NOT** aiming to have an overweight dog.

So, Bozo's standing outside the crate. "What's next?" he wonders (and you probably do, too). Easy.

Let him watch you as you scatter a small handful of kibble in the crate. Then close the door with Bozo on the outside. Guaranteed, he'll paw the door 'asking' to go in.

Open the door and let him in to eat the kibble. Close the door for 10 seconds. Repeat this process for each meal on Day 1. (That's four times.)

On Day 2, at lunchtime, close the door for a minute. It's unlikely that Bozo will protest. If he does, wait until he stops making noise (if only for two seconds!) and open the door immediately. Under NO circumstances should you open the door while Bozo is fussing. You will want to gradually increase the 'closed-door' times.

Feed him part of each of his next two meals for Day 2 in the crate with the door open.

Try closing the door again first meal on Day 3.

General Rule of Training:

If you move past the level of Bozo's acceptance or understanding, back up to the previously tolerated step (i.e. eating inside the crate with the door open). If you force him, he'll do it for sure but you will lose valuable trust and respect that will hinder teaching all future behavior.

Back in the chapter "He's Home. The Early Days", I suggested getting half a dozen or so stuffable chewtoys. These are specific purpose toys. With these you will develop Bozo Pup's acceptable object-chewing habit. Chewing is a natural behaviour for puppies. You will want to indulge that behaviour and enable him to form acceptable chewing habits. Squeaky toys, stuffed toys and balls are other use toys. Stuffed chewtoys are always to be considered 'settling tools' and ought not to be used other than in the crate, on Bozo Pup's bed or in the long-term confinement area.

Okay, so you got the chewtoys. Now...what are you supposed to put in them?

🐕 In one or two of these, put moistened kibble with a very small liver treat somewhere in the middle. Freeze them.

🐕 Stuff a couple more with dry kibble for easier removal. You can use canned dog food, a dab of honey or peanut butter to 'glue' the kibble in, if you choose.

I had a complaint recently that pup wasn't interested in his stuffed chewtoy. I checked and the kibble was so tightly stuffed in there, the poor little fellow lost interest after several minutes with no success.

Success is the key to moving forward—always.

Within the first week, Bozo is having all or part of his meals in the crate with the door closed. Hand feed the other half of the kibble, asking him to 'sit', 'come', or 'down'. Oops! I'm ahead of myself. Just hand feed the other half for now.

Bozo has now had part of his meal in the crate, been hand fed part and you want him back in the crate so you can move him somewhere in the house where you need to be.

Let him watch you toss in 2 or 3 stuffed chewtoys and close the door. Let him in when he asks. Close the door and move the crate.

Always be sure to put several stuffed chewtoys in the crate with Bozo. We want him to have positive association with his 'safe place'.

Chewing is a natural behavior for puppies. We need to indulge that behavior and enable him to form acceptable chewing habits.

Squeaky toys, stuffed toys & balls are "other use' toys. Stuffed chewtoys are always settling tools and ought not to be used other than in the crate, on his bed or in the long-term confinement area.

OK, so Bozo's in his crate chewing on his toy or perhaps napping. Now what? Set the timer for the top of the hour. When the timer goes, hustle Bozo to his outside toilet area.

Praise and treat for performance If no performance, return to his crate for ½ hour—by Day 2 you'll have this one down pat and Bozo will be getting the idea too.

You don't have a crate. You don't want a crate. You don't like crates. OK, no big deal.

Buy a flat dog cushion/bed.

In the various places you'll want him to be with you when you're at home, screw a hook or eyebolt big enough to attach his leash to, into the baseboard. Put a smaller eyebolt next to it to attach his stuffed chewtoy. This method also works.

Do **NOT** leave Bozo unattended while tied. You can't imagine how quickly puppies can tie themselves up and cause themselves harm. This method is for the vigilant.

Of course, it can be used in conjunction with crating, say beside your TV watching chair. Confinement and timing are the keys to successful potty training.

Oh, oh, the weekend is over. Vacation has ended. You all now have to be gone all day.

Now, what?

STORYTIME

· · · · · · · · · · · · ·

GUS THE GREETER

I don't always answer the phone. Living in family community, as I do, there are five other people ready to pounce on a ringing phone. So, let them have at it, I say.

One evening last week, I heard the phone ring, heard my son-in-law, Lee, answer it, after a brief conversation, I heard him say, "Thanks, Carol," and I continued reading. Just moments later Lee appeared in my doorway to say, "Meggie is gone. That was Carol. They put Meggie down today."

I let the tears come as lovely Meggie's image appeared. A Lab/Newf cross, she was a hefty girl with infinite patience and a touch of humor. We all loved her and my dog Jack, in his younger years, was totally smitten with her. She would carry a ball in her mouth all day, laying it down beside the bowl to have a drink or eat dinner. Then she'd pick it up again and wander off.

"Meggie's gone," I thought. "I'll miss her." I reached for a tissue to blow my nose and wipe my eyes.

In that moment, Gus' spirit showed up. Gus was my younger dog who left us three years ago (way too soon, I might add) at age eight. "Don't worry, Mom," he says to me now. "I've got her." I couldn't help but smile as I visualized large lumbering Meggie and bouncy Gus, both restored to their wholeness, cavorting on the other side of Rainbow Bridge.

"Do the girls know about Meggie?" I asked my oldest granddaughter, Lily, as we assembled at the dinner table the next night. "What about Meggie?" two little voices asked...almost as one. "They had to put Meggie down," replied Lily. I watched the girls' faces as the information landed. Sadness passed over Georgia's face. I saw it settle in. Sidney's head lowered and her eyes filled with tears.

"Y'know, girls," I said, "I was sad too when your Dad told me the news and I cried. We all loved Meggie. Then Gussy appeared to me and told me not to be sad because Meggie is with him now.

'Do you meet all The Dog House dogs when they cross Rainbow Bridge?' I asked him. 'I do,' he replied. That made me feel better. Maybe it will help you feel better too." A smile teased the corners of Sid's mouth.

"Boy, he's had a busy year, then," says Mom Heidi, "Wren, Jamieson, Chelsa, Antonio."

"Yes, and Bud," the girls added.

Gus the Greeter. I always knew he was destined for great things.

THE HOMECOMING...YOURS

Okay... so the family returns (either together or one at a time) and Bozo goes bananas. He barks, jumps up, and launches himself at the gate of his confinement area. As difficult as it is not to meet his energy with your own high-pitched greeting, especially if there are kids involved, **please don't.**

Right now—today—on your very first homecoming: Let's show Bozo how we'd like him to greet us.

Trust me, this is tough! Seems simple enough, I know, but it's tough to do. I know you want to run in, and scoop him up (and who wouldn't?) but believe me...a little restraint here will pay off big time in the long run.

Success in this, as with everything, will require a strategy:

Have some kibble or tiny pieces of liver treats in your pocket (and this goes for everyone, if there are several of you). You can keep some in your car or in a jar in the garage so you can always be 'armed.' Go into Bozo's area and stand quietly. In a second or two he will stop jumping and barking very briefly. In that **instant**, praise and treat and proceed to greet him however you choose.

Pick him up, get down on the floor with him, or put on his collar & leash and take him outside (a very good idea, incidentally). If several of you are returning at once, it would be very helpful if each person followed the same greeting ritual. I know it's a lot to ask but you'll be so pleased with the results in a few days. It really is worth it!

The goal: You are waiting for no barking and 'four on the floor' before you greet Bozo. It will be **really tough** not to match his enthusiastic greeting with your own but it's really important **NOT** to.

This is a critical first step in teaching Bozo basic good manners when greeting people. Like all training, it is important that you incorporate this into your daily activities. For example: when you let Bozo out of his crate, wait for that **moment of quiet** before you fuss him up.

Okay...so now is a good time to take Bozo to his outdoor toilet. Remember to praise and treat for performance. This is a great time to spend with Bozo. If he's 'empty,' he could do a little exploring inside, 100% supervised, of course, or a few minutes of training... sit, down, come (all this, of course, using part of his daily ration of kibble). Holding and handling now is also good...touching his feet, checking his teeth, fondling his ears, touching his rear end and genitals. Playing with his squeaky toys or tug of war are also options. Remember to have lots of brief 'time-outs.' The object here is to give Bozo some supervised freedom and social interaction after a long day alone and to ensure that you create the space for 'Bozo time' with this newest member of your family.

At dinnertime, Bozo is, for the time being, back in his crate with a stuffed chewtoy. Perhaps for variety or more interest, you might put a little cheese or peanut butter in his 'dinner time' chewtoy.

When the timer goes at the top of the hour, out he goes, with you, to his outdoor toilet. Once again, if he's empty, exploration time can follow. If you are a family, toileting Bozo can be assigned to different family members. It seems no one is super keen to go out in the freezing cold or pouring rain.

Pat yourself on the back for a successful Day 1 of Home Alone!

FEEDING BOZO

Like babies, puppies have small holding tanks (their stomachs!) and grow very quickly...as much as twenty times more quickly than adult dogs. Feeding Bozo can become somewhat of an issue. Who feeds him? What do I feed him...and when? Where? How Much? It's all a bit much, really. These questions, however, are all-important and need to be answered.

What?

A reputable breeder will most likely give you a bag of good quality puppy food to take home with your new puppy. Other puppy sources will probably not. In any event, you must always read the list of contents on the bag. The first ingredient should **always** be meat. Yes, you'll pay more for a good quality kibble but you'll feed less of it and you'll know that Bozo is getting the nutrients he needs to grow up strong and healthy. Personally, I wouldn't choose a kibble that contains any form of corn. You can decide this for yourself.

Feeding Bozo a raw diet is becoming more widely accepted. I feed my dog, Jack, raw food and have done for most of his life. Should you take this route, you'll need to research the amounts and kinds of supplements to add to the food to ensure a complete and nutritious diet and then use plain common sense. I like Dr. Ian Dunbar's comment on the subject of raw food vs. kibble: "After they're a year old, feed them anything you like."

For most of us, there's quite enough to do in those early weeks without having to prepare puppy food. With **good quality kibble** you've got both an excellent training reward and nutritious sustaining food. Remember to measure one day's ration into a container every day.

When?

Until Bozo is 4 months old (16 weeks), he needs to eat 4 times a day. From 4 to 6 months (16-20 weeks), he needs to eat 3 times a day. The easiest (and best) meal to eliminate is lunch. After 6 months, feed Bozo twice daily usually for life. My old Jack, now nearly 13, went from once a day a year ago back to twice a day in the past six months. That's his choice and privilege. He's earned it!

What goes in comes out, right? That means it's important for successful potty training to feed at approximately the same time every day.

KNOW THIS:

Free feeding a puppy is a sure way to cause in-house accidents. I say, "Don't."

If there's no one at home at lunchtime for that first four weeks, maybe a puppy-loving friend or neighbour can help out. If not, try the dog walking service in your area. If none of that works for you, make sure Bozo's lunch ration is stuffed in the chewtoys you'll be leaving for him.

How?

You may have noticed the absence of a food dish in this list of things I've recommended. That's because unless you're doing a food bowl exercise—more on that later—Bozo will be eating his meals either from your hand or a stuffed chewtoy. A handfed puppy learns many good things quickly (i.e. an inhibited bite and, most importantly, that human hands = good things!) Children often enjoy feeding puppies in this manner and it's a great occupation for both of them—supervised, of course!

Now that we've looked at what, when, and how to feed Bozo...let's move on to the all-important questions of where, who, and how much.

Where?

Have you given any thought as to exactly where will you feed Bozo? We've already talked about:

- using stuffed chewtoys in his crate or long-term confinement area;

- using bits of kibble as training rewards.

  Simple answer? Bozo can be fed anywhere... anywhere you're trying to teach him something, that is.

- *sit* by the door before you open it;

- *down* beside your chair;

- *take it/leave it in* the kitchen.

  "What? For his whole life?" you ask. Not at all.

By the time Bozo is 16-weeks-old he can be eating **most** of his dinner from a bowl. You will want to keep some kibble bits aside for ongoing training. When you get to this point, you might want to consider changing his training reward to something of higher value...a tasty tidbit of chicken or cheese, or maybe even a squeaky toy or ball.

Who?

Simple. Everyone. Especially if Bozo is to be a family companion. This includes visitors who can be given a few pieces of kibble or other treat when they arrive and instructed to feed them to Bozo when he approaches them. If you've taught *sit*, this is an excellent time to reinforce it by having visitors ask for a *sit* before giving the kibble/treat.

Toddlers love to feed puppies. Place the toddler's hand containing the kibble on your flat palm while you're both sitting on the floor. Ask the toddler to open her fist, keeping her fingers very still, and let Bozo eat the kibble. You need to stay **very** focused during this process as a nip from Bozo at this point can destroy a potentially beautiful relationship. Do I need to add here that toddlers and puppies should **never** be left unsupervised? Older kids can be taught the flat palm method too...an excellent opportunity to have them teach the *take it/leave it* exercise! Have I mentioned that kids are great puppy trainers? Show them the way you want it done, have them demonstrate to you that they get it, and they will produce excellent results. You'll be amazed!

How much?

Ultimately, you, as the adult are responsible for seeing that Bozo gets the correct amount of kibble each day. So, how much should you feed him? Read the feeding instructions on the bag of kibble and observe your puppy. For the most part, the bag's guidelines will be fine. Over time, you may need to make alterations. You should be able to *feel* your puppy's ribs, not *see* them. If you can't feel them, reduce his food ration. Obesity is just as unhealthy in dogs as it is in humans.

Varying Bozo's Diet

There are many who believe that dogs like variety in their diet (why wouldn't they?) and I am inclined to agree. If and when you decide to change Bozo's diet, and I certainly don't recommend doing it before eight months of age, be sure to do it gradually. Over the period of a week, gradually mix in a little of the new food with the old, increasing the amount each day so that by the end of the week, the switch has been made.

Water

It is critical that Bozo has access to fresh, clean water **at all times**. A huge responsibility...but the task can be made much easier if you consider an automatic water dispenser. These come in a wide variety of sizes and you will find them at most pet supply stores. I love them! No chance of tipping and less time spent refilling a water bowl.

So there you have it...a lot of talk about food and feeding. Because feeding provides so many training and rewarding opportunities and because the process is so extremely vital to Bozo's health and well being throughout his lifetime, I've had a lot to say on the subject. I hope you find it helpful.

WHY BOTHER WITH TRAINING

· ·

Don't I have enough to do already?

So far, we've talked about potty training, confinement, your homecoming at the end of the day, and feeding. Isn't all that enough?

Look at this cute little puppy. Surely he'll grow up to be a well behaved dog if we're nice to him, won't he? Miracles do happen, I agree. But I wouldn't count on that. Unless you teach (train) your puppy to behave the way you want him to, it will take a miracle to have acceptable behavior happen.

Let's talk about training...

I've heard people say that they didn't want to train their dog because they didn't want a robot...that training, apparently, would stifle Bozo's enthusiasm and zest. Reasonable, I guess, (I don't believe this) but several questions come immediately to mind.

Do you really want a dog who:

🐾 barks at everyone who visits your home?

🐾 jumps boisterously at/on everyone, including small children?

endangers his own life by dashing away instead of coming when called?

Probably not. Hopefully not.

What you decide to teach your dog is your call. All trainers will have a list of things that they think your dog should learn. Admittedly, I do, too, but ultimately, you need your dog to know whatever it takes to have him fit into *your* lifestyle. If potty training plus *come, sit, stay*, and *off* are all you need, that's great. This said, I truly believe that dogs love learning. More than this, many require it in order to avoid the establishment of destructive habits that come from simply being bored. It seems a shame to not take advantage of their ability to learn...but still, it's your call.

I once heard Dr. Ian Dunbar say, "If your dog is perfect for you, he's perfect." True, I guess, as long as you're never leaving Bozo with anyone else, never leaving him in a daycare or boarding situation, or ever having friends or family come visit. Will that be the case? Probably not.

There are many methods of training. The old 'jerk & push' methods don't merit mention except to say there are more effective, easier gentle methods widely available now. The two methods I particularly like are clicker training and lure training.

I think clicker training is great. By this method, desirable behaviour is marked by using a "clicker," a mechanical device that makes a short, distinct "click" sound, which tells the animal exactly when they're doing the right thing. With the click, a trainer can precisely "mark" behaviour so that the animal knows exactly what it was doing. Check out Karen Pryor's website for more information (www.karenpryoracademy.com).

Maybe because I am not the most hand/eye co-coordinated person in the world, I think lure training is easier for the new puppy owner—one less thing for your hand & eye to manage.

As Dr Ian Dunbar says (frequently and with great emphasis), the science of lure training is pure and simple...as simple, in fact, as 1–2–3–4:

1. Request
2. Lure
3. Response
4. Reward.

For example:

1. Say, "Sit."

2. Lure the dog to sit by moving a food lure upwards in front of the dog's nose, so that:

3. As the dog raises his head to follow the food, he compensates by lowering his rump to the ground and sits—the desired Response, and so:

4. Reward the dog with a scratch behind his ear, by throwing a ball or stick to retrieve, or by simply just giving him the food.

KNOW THIS:

It is important to phase out the food reward very quickly. *Quickly* means with 20 repetitions.

Regardless of which method you use, and I'm not advocating any method other than those I've mentioned, **timing** is of the essence. Dogs read body language far more quickly than they understand language. What is rewarded will be repeated. **Be careful what you reward.**

To illustrate:

You are teaching Bozo to *sit*. Your allergies have been acting up this week and you're sneezing a lot. Every time you say *sit* you sneeze. This goes on for a day or two. When the sneezing stops, don't be surprised if Bozo no longer sits when he hears *sit*. Not a big deal. Just restart the *sit* training

Incorporate what you want to teach Bozo into your daily routine—training is much easier that way and you do not have to set aside chunks of time specifically to teach Bozo manners.

For example:

- have Bozo *sit* before putting on or taking off his collar and/or leash;

- have him *sit* before feeding or going through a door;

- have him *sit* before you or visitors greet him;

- have him *sit* before you cross the street on a walk.

A word of caution: If at any time when you are training and Bozo refuses a treat, stop the session immediately and give him a break. He is either stressed, tired, or overwhelmed.

Are you getting the idea?

Sit is probably the most useful behavior you can teach Bozo. Once he has demonstrated a reliable *sit*, so many things become preventable: jumping on family/visitors, dashing through the door, begging at the table...the list goes on and on.

If you can't decide what or how much you want to teach your puppy, at least, I implore you, teach him to **sit**.

HANDLING

Hugging and Restraint

Hugging and handling...sounds like a no-brainer, right? I mean, doesn't everyone want to pick up a puppy and hug it? So how do you figure puppies feel about it? Do they love it? Your guess is as good as mine. Other than for the sheer joy of it, puppies need to be hugged and handled as much as possible for their own future good and yours too. Visits to the vet, grooming, and toenail clipping will all require considerable handling, so your best bet is to get Bozo comfortable with the idea right away. Like everything else involved with training the newest member of your family, there's a proper way to go about this as well.

While you are seated, pick Bozo up and hook your finger in his collar, holding him gently, but firmly, to you. Run your free hand from the top of his head down his back, speaking to him quietly and soothingly. After a few moments (and a kiss on his nose, if you like) turn him on his back, touching his chest with your fingertips. Humming a little tune can be helpful here, and may increase Bozo's sense of relaxation. Massage his belly and groin area with your palm and fingertips, working your way down each hind leg to the feet. Handle the toes on each of his four feet foot separately...briefly at first, but over time increase to a minute or so per foot.

Think calm. Stay calm. If Bozo struggles or becomes vocal, do **not** release him. Calmly massage him until he is quiet and then let him go using your release word (*okay/all done* or whatever word you have opted to use). If he has struggled, I strongly suggest that you repeat this exercise within the next ten minutes or so. If all goes quietly and you now have a relaxed, limp puppy, have a look in his ears (both of them), open his mouth and run a finger along the outside of his teeth, touch his rear end and his private bits.

You may or may not need treats for this exercise. It's the hands = good things message that we're trying to impart here. This said, feel free to use a few anyway, telling Bozo what a good lad he is.

KNOW THIS:

Bozo can both read your body language and sense when you are stressed. The key is to remain calm.

Hum and gentle tune, speak quietly, and breathe deeply. Take your time. This is important bonding time for you both.

Once Bozo is 'four on the floor' again, briefly handle each of his four feet before releasing him to go play or chew a stuffed Kong ®. Alternating play sessions and calming sessions is a good idea. As a rule, dogs do not generalize very well so handling sessions should be planned for a variety of places in your home. Be sure to include the whole family in this activity. You will want to supervise young children to make sure that these sessions remain calming and not turn into high-energy playtime. There'll be lots of time for that! Willing visitors can also be included in this activity. I would, in fact, encourage them to participate. They represent the future strangers (vet, groomer, etc.) in Bozo's life. Start with adult family, then children, and gradually add visiting women, men, and children in that order. We're aiming to have Bozo enjoy being handled, not simply tolerate it.

The Brush

Within a couple of days of beginning the handling exercise, introduce a brush. Place the brush on the floor and let Bozo sniff and investigate it. Talk to him encouragingly while he does and reward him with a treat. The first time you pick up the brush, make one gentle motion down his back with it. Say, "Yes, Bozo!" and give him a treat. Continue for a couple of additional strokes if he seems to be doing okay. Again, praise and treat. Now, put the brush away. It's the old 'leave 'em wanting more' trick. Over the course of a week, increase the time gradually until you can brush him lightly all over his body.

The Toenail Clippers

Few things tend to inspire terror in dogs more than toenail clippers. This is not necessary. After you've been handling Bozo's feet for a couple of days, try a variation of the routine we used with introducing him to the brush.

Put the clippers on the floor where he can check them out. When he does, say, "Yes, Bozo!" and give him a treat. End of session.

The next session, after he checks them out, pick up the clippers and click them in the air. "Yes, Bozo!"/treat. End of session.

Next time, touch a toe or two with the clippers. "Yes, Bozo!"/treat for each toe. End of session.

The next time, clip a tiny bit off, say, two toenails. ""Yes, Bozo!"/treat for each toe. End of session.

This process should continue until all of Bozo's toenails have been clipped. Although it may seem a long process to you for just one small thing, it can be accomplished over a day or two...and trust me on this, it will pay big dividends in the end. If Bozo is a regularly-walked city dog concrete and asphalt help wear down his toenails so less frequent trimming is necessary. If not, toenail clipping becomes a life-long activity for you. The method I suggest will make it easy and enjoyable for both of you.

STORYTIME

. . . .

The Best of the Best

For Sale: Male Valley Bulldog puppy, 9 weeks old. Will grow to 55 lbs. 999-5555

"Hmm," I thought, reading the ad in the local paper. "I wonder what a Valley Bulldog is." As I heard the door close, I called out, "Neil, what's a Valley Bulldog?"

"I don't know," he said. "Is there a phone number?"

"Yup."

"Want me to call?"

"Okay."

Within ten minutes we were driving to 'see' this puppy. If you are a dogless dog lover, who is 'thinking' about getting a puppy, going to 'see' a puppy is extremely dangerous! The puppy seller was not at home when we arrived but a small freckle-faced boy indicated the puppies were 'in there' pointing to the open back door. Just then, a shoebox size pup appeared in the doorway. Confident and curious, his bully-stance asked, "Is someone looking for me?"

I was smitten. Nearly all white with a perfect dark brindle circle above his tail and a dark brindle mask, this cocky youngster 'had me at hello.' Seriously.

Young Freckle Face seemed to be the in-charge salesman, at least for the moment. Starting his pitch, he informed me "Mom wants a lot of money for him, you know."

"Oh," I said. "How much?"

"Three dollars, "he replied.

"That is a lot of money," I agreed, mentally adding a couple of zeros.

Waiting for Mom to come home, Neil and I chatted as we strolled, puppy-in-arms, through the long grass on the property, noting the Mastiff pacing back and forth in a large pen.

From nowhere, I felt a tug on the hem of my jacket. I moved puppy in my arms to better see the source of the tug.

"Missus," says Freckle Face, "his name is Jack."

"Oh, okay," I say. "Thanks." Jack? That is not the name I would have chosen...but who am I to argue with a six year old?"

Solid, dependable, kind, independent, polite... if 'Jack' means all these things, then this puppy was well named.

A couple of hours later, following the required negotiation and payment procedures (as though that really was an issue!) and having met the other available Valley Bull pup (a shy black & white female), Neil and I had Jack in the car on the way to his forever home.

Now, nearly thirteen years later, kidneys failing and joints crippled with arthritis, Jack is still the best of the best. Hands down.

Impulse? Sure. Regret? Never. I continue to love every second I have with him.

SOCIALIZATION...PEOPLE

. . . .

Have a puppy party. In fact, have several of them during the first month Bozo comes to live with you.

"A what? You mean put lots of puppies in one place together?" No, not quite. Not yet.

This is a concept I first heard from Dr. Ian Dunbar. I love the idea so here it is. Based on Dunbar's premise that a puppy needs to meet at least 100 **different** people in his first 12 weeks, the puppy party concept is a fun way to accomplish this while beefing up your own social life as well. Neat, huh?

Teaching a puppy to love people...all people—friends, strangers, big, small...and to be super sociable is so important to his enjoyment of life and yours. Why would anyone even want a family companion who doesn't like people?

So here's the deal. Bozo has arrived at your house. Family, friends & neighbors are clamoring to meet him. Great! Let's get the biggest possible bang for your buck, though, by having all visitors follow a few simple rules. For his first couple of visitors, I'd recommend inviting only one or two *dog-savvy* children (closely supervised). You can build from there.

Now, about that Puppy Party...

"Oh, he's so cute! I love puppies," says your next-door neighbour as she reaches down to pick up Bozo, who already has his paws on her kneecaps. "Please, don't," you say. "Wait until he has 'four on the floor' for an instant, then you can pick him up."

Ideally, of course, you've gone over a few ground rules before the introduction. In the *real* world, that's not so likely to be the way things go.

Primarily, the 3 major things that we want to accomplish are:

1. Having Bozo meet lots of different people

2. Letting Bozo be picked up only after he has 'four on the floor'

3. Having Bozo hugged (restrained) by all visitors

For starters, invite a few (or a lot...you decide) of your girlfriends over for wine, conversation, tea and crumpets—whatever works best for you. Tell them why you're doing this and demonstrate the hugging and handling techniques you'd like them to employ as they arrive. Give everyone a small bag of kibble... from Bozo's daily ration, of course. Play *Pass the Puppy* with everyone hugging and holding Bozo...touching all his body parts, and giving lots of praise and kibble rewards.

Do this a couple or three times in the first four weeks Bozo is with you. In addition, invite a group of men over to watch a game...hockey is good. You can lure them, no doubt, with the promise of beer and snacks. Encourage them, as though they'll need it, to make lots of noise and between periods, after you have supplied them with small bags of kibble and explained what you want, they can play *Pass the Puppy*. Same rules as above apply.

Bozo needs to meet kids too. I suggest keeping a kids' group small. You will need to be able to supervise all of them at once. Before they meet Bozo, have a little chat with them explaining the 'ouch' when Bozo's sharp teeth touch their skin and the 'stand tall like a tree' when Bozo jumps up. After they meet Bozo, sit with them and show them the calming massage and the feet fondling. Encourage the children to be gentle. Set them up in pairs, each with a bag of kibble, and show them how to play "Bozo, come" in, say, a 6–8 foot space. Playtime is fun, but Bozo needs rules...so call timeouts frequently and let the game resume. Puppy parties with kids are fun, entertaining for adults, and high energy. I recommend a helper!

For the second kids' party (assuming you're brave enough to do this twice) have balloons, hats for the kids to put on, noisemakers, and toys, such as friction floor cars. This is another excellent opportunity for Bozo to encounter new and strange things.

It's easy enough to use kibble to get Bozo to *come*, *sit*, or *down* and *come* is so easy when there's more than one person. We haven't talked about any of those things yet, have we?

In short...

Start working with Bozo's *come*, *sit* and grabbing his **collar as soon as you get him home.**

Give visiting family, friends, and neighbors the basic rules **befor**e they meet Bozo.

One dog-savvy child in the first couple of days; **never** a large number and supervise at all times.

Have puppy parties for women, men, and children, in that order. 100 different people in 12 weeks is easy if you use **every opportunity**.

SOCIALIZATION...THINGS

When I started writing this section, I made a list of things, to which Bozo ought to be exposed, I thought. It didn't take me long to realize that such a list is almost endless. Whatever you can dream up is a 'thing' for Bozo. You just need to remember that absolutely everything is new to him. Put yourself in his place. Stand in any room in your home and see, smell, and hear the things as though you had never experienced them before. In the kitchen, for example, the sound of a mixer came immediately to mind. As you expose Bozo to these new things, be careful not to scare him. That's why younger is better. Until they reach adolescence (5-6 months of age), they accept new experiences readily. As with people, puppy adolescence brings a wariness of all things new.

Never force your puppy to investigate. This is an adventure, not boot camp!

Probably the first sound Bozo is likely to hear is the doorbell or knock on the door. Training opportunity! If he barks at the knock or the bell, you can say, "Thank you, Bozo" as you both head for the door. Before you open it, say, "Bozo, sit." When he does, say, "Yes, treat."

(Remember to keep treats on your person at all times!) Depending on how bouncy, Bozo is, you may need to repeat this several times. I think the key here is to focus on Bozo's sitting and not be impatient to open the door. Whoever is there will most probably wait and you don't want to miss this training opportunity! After several attempts, if you get the *sit* but not the *stay*, either pass Bozo off to another family member or simply scoop him up, saying nothing. He has done nothing wrong. He's just learning. The door thing is such a big deal because it involves noise, people, barking, and the potential for bolting (Bozo's). DO take the time to develop and foster the behavior you want. Focusing on Bozo now for a few weeks will make a lifetime of difference. It would be great if a visitor or a family member would help with this exercise by knocking or ringing to come in and then coming in and going out (maybe by another door) and repeating the knock, ring, bark, *sit*, open door. Part Two of this exercise one is to remind the visitor not to speak to Bozo until he has 'four on the floor.'

In these early weeks, take Bozo to the mall...or anywhere else, for that matter, where he'll experience a whole new array of different sights, sounds, and smells all at once. Carry him in your arms and stop and chat with everyone you know (and anyone else who wants to meet your new family member). Hats, headscarves, big purses, beards, sunglasses, umbrellas, skateboards, tricycles, strollers, wheelchairs, walkers, and canes are all things that Bozo is likely to encounter. Why not make a list? Don't be limited by my ideas! Check off each new experience as you move through your list.

Encourage, praise and reward the lad. Never push... and keep the time periods short. Stop immediately if Bozo seems worried or stressed. Enroll visiting friends and family by having them wear hats, beards, costumes, and so on. Seems like a lot of thought on your part, right? You bet. Not only does it have the potential to be fun, though: you are laying the foundation for a 'bomb-proof' dog in just a few short weeks.

Two helpful things to remember if Bozo is apprehensive when you introduce him to new things:

1. keep his focus on you with positive vocal reinforcement and treats; and

2. position yourself between Bozo and anything he might find scary.

SOCIALIZATION...PLACES

It may be too soon for puppy class and the dog park but outings are still important. Using the crate in the car is important too, for his safety and yours. Once Bozo has learned a reliable *sit,stay* and *settle* , you can teach him those cues in your *stationary* car (more on that later).

Starting with short rides, a quick trip for milk or a hop to pick up the mail, put Bozo in his crate in the back seat and take him along. He probably had one car ride to get to you. Don't stop now. The more you take him, the more accustomed he'll be; therefore the less likelihood of carsickness.

If you think bringing him into the corner store *in your arms* would be allowed, by all means, do it and encourage anyone who wants to pet him. The more new people, the better, remember? Of course, this adds minutes to your errand. This is your time investment in your newest family member; the dividends are huge.

Everything we do with Bozo starts small (brief periods) and gradually grows larger (longer periods) By all means, as time moves on, leave him crated or settled in the car while you pick up your groceries, say, 40 minutes, but only if it's neither freezing cold or boiling hot. In any case, put a blanket in Bozo's crate for the cooler weather car rides. Jack now enjoys a hot water bottle under the blanket on his back seat... comforting warmth for arthritic joints.. Always leave at least one car window open a bit—it's a no-brainer to say, the warmer the weather, the wider the window (s) need to open. When the temperature is above 20 degrees Celsius, leave him at home

Anywhere you can carry Bozo, it's a good idea to take him. If you have friends who would welcome a visit from Bozo, take him with you to their house. For everyone's peace of mind, be sure to follow the same guidelines as at your house; bring in the crate, keep Bozo in it, take him outside at the top of the hour and only an empty Bozo is permitted supervised exploration. By now, stuffed chewtoys and confinement are a habit for both of you. If you give Bozo a potty opportunity on the way in, everyone will have a more relaxed, fun visit.

Perhaps you are fortunate, as I was, and you are able to bring Bozo to work. When my Jack was just a lad, I was Catering Manager at a hotel. I worked crazy, long hours, often in the hotel until after 3 a.m. Luckily, I had an office so on those late nights, I took Jack, his crate, chewtoys, his water bowl, and a gate and set him up in my office. The catering staff provided a steady stream of visitors, some of whom volunteered to take him outside for a potty break. All those strange people, new smells, and different objects served Jack well in his early socialization. Perhaps, you too, can take Bozo to your office occasionally.

Many vets advise against exposing puppies to other dogs and /or areas frequented by dogs until the immunity created by their regimen of vaccinations is adequate... generally by three months. Once this deadline is reached, you can begin leash walks around the neighborhood, stopping of course to meet and greet all interested folks. Remember to take kibble and ask people to wait for the 'four on the floor' before greeting your enthusiastic pup. If you've been in the habit of taking a power walk around the block yourself, you'll want to make that a separate item on your daily agenda now.

The benefit of dog ownership kicks in. Slow down and smell the roses. Bozo will!

Now, too, you can sign up for puppy classes and take Bozo to the dog park. Try to choose a time at the dog park when there aren't tons of dogs there. Be vigilant, but for the most part, let him make his own way. If there are signs of bullying by the older, bigger dogs, especially if there are several of them—growling, teeth baring, forward aggressive stance—pick up Bozo and leave. In my experience, that's rare. Dogs left to themselves will generally sort out who's who. Mostly you just need to stand by and watch.

Did I mention... you will meet really neat dog lovers like yourself at the dog park. **Bonus!**

SOCIALIZATION...EXPLORATION

Whatever is in his immediate environment such as carpet, grass, flooring, pavement, cement and gravel will probably become familiar to Bozo within a few days of your bringing him home. Surfaces like ice, beach rocks or sand you may want to introduce eventually. Then again, maybe you won't. The only reason I mention this is so YOU won't be surprised if Bozo balks at walking on any strange surface.

KNOW THIS:

The more you expose him to, the better it will be in the long run.

At home, you can have him walk over a garbage bag taped to the floor—this is an excellent opportunity for kids, who can make a game of "Come, Bozo" across the bag and then back again in exchange for rewards. A ladder laid on the ground makes an interesting obstacle course and can be hysterically funny depending on Bozo's size and level of curiosity. A piece of mesh, a coconut mat, a rubber bathtub mat, slippery wet decking—anything that you can think of to lay on the floor or ground or that is already a horizontal surface—can provide a new adventure for Bozo. That said, **never** force him; if he balks, simply remove him or the thing that appears to be causing consternation and try it again at another time.

Objects on surfaces are interesting to our intrepid explorer too. Big balls like soccer or beach balls are fun to explore if they're introduced before Bozo reaches the wariness of adolescence. Be gentle in moving the ball. Don't try to hit him with it.

Mopping a floor using a bucket and a string or fibre mop can be more fun than you ever imagined! If the gig is to get the floor clean quickly and efficiently, introduce Bozo to the mop, have him watch it move slowly once or twice, then ask him to *leave i*t and lure him away with a treat. If you want this to be more fun and perhaps even entice the kids to mop the floor—less quickly and less cleanly, granted—allow Bozo to chase the mop, stopping the game at frequent intervals with a *leave it*. C'mon now, how clean does the floor really have to be?

A tunnel made of one or two cardboard boxes (or even three, once Bozo gets the idea) can provide hours of entertainment and exploration value, especially if there are pieces of kibble inside. Just one cardboard box with a hole in the side and a tasty reward inside provides another anti-boredom activity. Wind-up toys can provoke a variety of reactions. If there are children in your life, exposing Bozo to small things that clatter their way across the floor is a very good idea.

The first time Bozo experiences a vacuum cleaner, it should be at least across the hall and, over time, moved closer to him. Many dogs have vacuum issues and while I get that (I, too, hate the noisy things!) it's both inconsiderate and unfair to condition Bozo to cower in a corner or to attack the vacuum every time it appears. They do tend to be used with great frequency, I find!

We'll end this exploration of surfaces with the stairs. Carpeted or rough textured ones are much easier and infinitely less scary for Bozo. My suggestion is to put him on stair #1 the first time; repeat several times. Praise and reward each time he comes down. Move through stairs #2, #3, and so on. Be sure to watch him carefully as he gets higher.

The more you take Bozo with you as you go about your routine, the more he encounters the unfamiliar in his daily life. That's a **good** thing.

STORYTIME

· · · · · · · · · · · · ·

Gus Joins the Family

"My brother will pick him up," I told the breeder, "and he'll have the shipping crate. How much does Gus weigh? The airline needs to know."

"Ten pounds...maybe six," she answered, unsure. "He's small for his age"

"OK, then. Gus will be picked up tomorrow. Thanks for everything."

Late the following evening, we could hear the high-pitched "yip, yip, yip" clear across the terminal building as we hurried to collect Gus who had just arrived in St. John's, NL from Halifax, NS. My second Valley Bulldog (Bull-Boxer) had arrived to join Jack...an 18-month-old worrier.

Up to that point, Jack had had a great life, but I worked full-time (always coming home at lunch hour to take him for a quick walk, mind you) and for the rest of the day, Jack essentially whiled away the hours on the couch, alone with the radio. I hoped Gus would cheer him up and be his buddy.

I wasn't sure how the introduction would go so my friend, Neil, came with me to facilitate this important meeting. Even then I knew that neutral territory is always the best bet for introductions but it was late at night and raining—not an inviting prospect.

The drive home was fine and as we walked into the house, Jack wriggled his staid self to greet us at the door, his whole body aquiver in his joy at seeing Neil, his dearest friend. "Hello, Wiggle Bum!" Neil greeted him as he put Gus on the floor.

Gus was every inch the puppy in his unabashed curiosity about Jack. Wriggling...bouncing...jumping. Jack sniffed Gus all over and turned his attention back to the humans. Neil and I smiled at one another. "Well, that went well, didn't it?" we laughed.

Moments later as we settled with tea and Jack was back on his couch, the 'new guy' put his two front paws on the couch where Jack was sitting and whimpered. Cautiously I lifted him up...waiting for the reaction. Reaction? A lifted head and a sniff from Jack as if to say, "Okay, kid" was all we got whereupon Gus promptly tucked himself into Jack's belly and went to sleep.

Night One. Done.

I was a little alarmed at breakfast time the next morning though, as I watched Gus make his way under Jack's belly and between his front legs to eat from his dish. Uh-oh. What do I do? Nothing. A knowledgeable friend once told me that there comes a time when we (humans) just have to back away and let the dogs sort it out amongst themselves...so I just watched. Unperturbed, Jack continued eating. I pretty much gave up any concerns right then.

There were to be lots of good times ahead as Gus continued to insert his bouncy Boxer energy into Jack's stolid Bully presence.

BITE INHIBITION

. . . .

"Puppies bite and thank goodness they do."

When I first read that in Dr. Ian Dunbar's book *After You Get Your Puppy*[2] I immediately remembered all the occasions when I've seen puppies severely reprimanded for doing what comes naturally to them. My curiosity aroused, I read on—and I recommend you do too—the book, I mean.

Janis Bradley's book, *Dogs Bite But Balloons and Slippers are More Dangerous* is a fascinating read especially if you'd like a more balanced perspective on the dog attack stories that unfold frequently in the media.

Puppies learn dog bite inhibition from their mothers and littermates. Using their mouths (i.e. biting) is their normal form of play. If one pup's teeth hurt another, you'll hear a yelp. If you're watching, you'll see a moment's break in play and then, back at it again. Unfortunately for us, they will tend to do the same with humans. This is where the "...and thank goodness they do..." comes in. By what method could we possibly

---

2 Go to www.dogstardaily.com where you will be able to download the free e-book.

teach them **how** to bite if they never bit at all? Why is it necessary for dogs to bite? Simple. It's their primary mechanism of defence. In fact, puppies that don't bite run the risk of growing to become adolescents and, eventually adults that are at great risk for receiving injury-causing bites.

There is no doubt that Bozo's needle sharp teeth cause pain. We'd all agree on that one. Fortunately for us, there's little strength in his young jaws. While his nipping may sting, he doesn't actually, as a puppy, have the power to do great damage. For now. what he needs to learn, however, is that his teeth are **never** to apply pressure to human skin and we need to make that message absolutely clear before he's 18 weeks (4 ½ months) old.

So how do we go about this? Easy.

Think about it. When Bozo bites one of his four-legged friends, they yelp. So when he decides to turn his teeth on you:

Say a loud, offended, "Ouch!" As he backs off, lean away from him for a short time out. Then invite him to *come*, *sit*, and lie *down*. That's his apology. Now you can resume play.

If Bozo doesn't back off when you 'yelp,' call him a Meanie or a Bully and leave the area for a few seconds (minutes as he gets older). Before long, he will connect the painful bite to your leaving. When you return, call him to you, have him *sit* and then once again...game on! His long-term confinement area is an excellent place to play with Bozo. When you need to leave him because he's not respecting your "Ouch!" he'll still in his 'safe place.'

Up to this point (say three months or so), Bozo's needle sharp teeth have no real force behind them, but as you continue to play, and in order to teach him to exert **NO** pressure, you need to pretend they do. Bozo needs to learn **not** to hurt people. It will be very important that you teach all visitors the 'ouch/lean away/time out' exercise explained above. Everyone will benefit.

The Concept of *Off*

Like the *Sit* command, *Off.* is a multi-use concept... and one that you will find to be invaluable.

Start with a food treat held out in your hand. When Bozo sniffs it, say,"Off." If he leaves it alone for **one second**, then you say, "Take it."

Repeat, repeat, repeat.

Then add another second before saying,"Take it." Gradually increase the number of seconds until you reach, say, a minute.

A variation of this is to put the food treat on a flat surface. Once Bozo sees it, shield it with your fingers, tent-like. Remove your fingers. If Bozo waits **one second**, say, "Take it" and proceed as above.

If Bozo touches the treat before you're ready, simply start again from one second. It won't take many repetitions for him to learn that he needs to hear, *take it* before he touches the treat.

Mouthing is its own reward for puppies so when playing the game, say *off* frequently. Praise when Bozo stops, then resume the mouthing game and only produce the food when the session is over.

Failure to heed your request results in the same action as the "ouch" earlier. Free your hand from Bozo's mouth, call him a Meanie or a Bully, mutter dire threats and leave the room for a minute or two. If the room has a door, shut it in his face. When you return after a few minutes, ask him to *come* and *sit* before resuming the game.

Once he understands the *off* request, you can transfer this skill to when Bozo is mouthing. Say *off;* waggle the food treat to entice him to let go. When he does, praise and treat

Play fighting and tug of war are excellent ways to maintain Bozo's soft mouth. You, the owner, need to have good control over your puppy and as long as you both 'play by the rules'[3] with lots of breaks in each play session, play fighting provides the opportunity for greater control, no matter how excited Bozo might get.

Puppies learn what we teach them. Often in puppy training, we humans need to learn as much as Bozo does. Be sure to review all the steps in your mind before you begin each session. That way you'll be clear about the exact behavior you wish to reward.

KNOW THIS:

Unless your puppy's mouth has regular contact with a human hand (usually and most often, your hand) he's bound to forget what he's learned and drift back to a hard bite. Hand feeding, teeth cleaning and regular behavior checks will provide the necessary reminders to him.

These are your keys to a biddable dog with an inhibited bite.

Have fun!

---

3 The rules: "Ouch!"; "Come."; "Sit."; "Off."; "Down."; Leaving the area; Frequent stops and starts."

JUMPING UP

. . . .

I had no idea how selfish I was being when other people's dogs would jump on me and I'd say, "Oh, that's okay...I don't mind." Wow! How thoughtless and inconsiderate!

What about big dogs, wet dogs, muddy dogs, and small, elderly, or fearful people? Is jumping on them okay, too? I think not...and I apologize to anyone whose dog training I interfered with. At those times, my love and enthusiasm for my doggy friends, apparently, overrode my common sense. As Maya Angelou says, "When we know better, we do better."

Now that I can see the ramifications of my behavior on your efforts to teach your dog good manners, I don't allow **any** puppy or dog to jump up. I think now is the right time to talk about how to teach your puppy this aspect of good manners (these are frequently important for people, too).

Puppies are excitable...puppies jump up on people! It's what they do, and it's quite normal for them. Of course, this is not completely true for humans. So how do we fix it? (Hint: If he's sitting, Bozo can't be jumping, right?)

KNOW THIS:

In these early days, ALWAYS have kibble or treats in your pocket. You will always be ready for action and can incorporate training into virtually every aspect of Bozo's day. I can't stress this enough.

So think about it...when is the first time Bozo jumps up on you on any given day? The first time he sees you, of course! The instant that his tiny (or not so tiny!) paws hit your leg, stand still, say nothing, and turn away. He will likely stop and look puzzled. Hold your position!

The minute he has "four on the floor," waggle a piece of kibble back and forth just over his nose. He will follow it. Give it to him.

With a second piece, move the kibble over the top of his nose between his eyes. Following it will cause his bum to find the floor...and the second it does, say, "Yes!" and give him the kibble.

Immediately repeat this two or three times, then add, "Sit!" before you move the kibble.

Spend a minute or two with him and before you put on his leash to take him to his outside toilet, do it again and say, "Sit!"

Move the treat back over Bozo's nose, when Bozo *sits*, you say "Yes!" and give the treat.

The sight of his leash may send Bozo into another jumping frenzy providing another perfect *sit* opportunity.

What if Bozo keeps jumping up on me when I turn away the first time? No worries. Hang in there!

Say **nothing**. Ignore him and be ready. He will stop eventually and when he does, be ready with the kibble/treat to lure him to *sit*.

Okay...so I can hear you now, "This will take me forever. I don't have time in the morning." Blah, blah, blah. Remember when I told you that the first eight to ten weeks would require a **huge** commitment? I wasn't lying. Your puppy is an investment...and the minutes you spend each day in the beginning will pay unimaginably huge dividends in the days, weeks, months, and years to come. It's all good...just stick with it! If need be, set your alarm a little earlier in the morning so that you can make the time and space needed for these few minutes of valuable training.

Bonus!

If you start this training from day one, Bozo will eventually be ready to properly greet *his first visitors.*

"I didn't even think of that," you say. "How so?"

Easy. Give each visitor a small bag of kibble as they come in (measured from Bozo's daily ration, of course) and explain to them what you want them to do and how important it is for them to not pay Bozo any attention until he *sits*. Be sure to get their agreement to do it **your** way before proceeding.

There now...you've just made a very important first step to having a well-mannered canine companion!

SIT

· · · ·

We've talked about *sit* quite a bit already. In fact, I have suggested that you teach Bozo to *sit* even if you teach him nothing else. It is so easy to teach a young puppy, though, that it seems crazy to me not to teach them as much as is possible. It's not only simple but it's fun. And the benefits? Limitless. But I digress...

Session 1

Get your bag of kibble (I would strongly suggest that you put a couple of pieces of liver treat in there for bonus rewards for super-fast responses or compliance in the face of distractions).

Give Bozo one piece of kibble to alert him that it's "Game on!"

Now take apiece of kibble. Waggle it in front of Bozo's nose, moving it low and slow back and forth over his nose between his eyes, saying, "Bozo, sit." As soon as his bum touches the floor, say, "Yes!" and give him the treat. Repeat this 3-5 times and that's it for this session. (You may have to move around a bit between *sits*. I've known puppies who *sit* the first time and then, knowing that you have treats, simply sit there and wait for more.)

Session 2

Later the same day:

Waggle a treat in front of Bozo and ask for a *sit*. When you get it...reward with a treat. On the second repetition, delay giving the treat by a second or two. The third time? Reward quickly. On the fourth repetition, ask for the *sit*, and instead of a food reward, offer praise: "Yes, good boy!" On the fifth repetition, ask for and get the *sit*, praise, and release. After release, (you can use any word that works for you—*okay...all done*...whatever) have a play session with a toy, roll around on the floor, or play tug of war... anything that's fun for both of you.

As you continue to ask for a *sit* throughout the day, give a food reward every now and then. Be sure they're **random**, and not simply on every 6th or 3rd or 5th request. If, at any time, you ask Bozo for a *sit* and Bozo does not comply, go back to square one (i.e. five requests, five rewards) and when you have a 100% success, move to step two. Do everything you can to set Bozo up for success.

Ultimately, *sit* becomes the canine equivalent of 'please' so use it whenever Bozo wants something.

If he wants out...ask for a *sit*. When he wants back in? Same thing.

Have Bozo *sit* to say hello to you and others.

Before you put his dinner bowl on the floor (after you've graduated from hand feeding, that is), ask for a *sit*.

Before you put his leash on him and before you take it off...before he jumps in the car, before you pick him up... and on and on. Before any activity, *sit* will become automatic for both of you.

In the end, the activity becomes the reward and by incorporating the *sit* request into your daily routine, you will find that it happens in a variety of places. Be sure to ask for *sit* outdoors too—while walking or playing. In these cases, resuming the walk or the game will be the reward.

When you have achieved 100% reliability, introduce a hand signal to indicate *sit*—extremely useful at a distance. How? Read on.

Standing a foot or two from Bozo, **BEFORE** you say "Bozo, *sit*." raise your hand from your side, palm open and turned upwards to about halfway between your thigh and your waist. **Then** say, "Bozo, *sit*." (The hand motion is rather like throwing a softball in an underhand pitch.)

From now on, before asking for a *sit,* do the hand signal. After half a dozen repetitions or so, try the hand signal only. If Bozo *sits*, be sure to offer lots of praise and a treat. This is a new thing, after all, and quite deserving of a reward. Again, as you gain reliability with the hand signal as the only cue, randomize the rewards. To increase reliability, alternate randomly the verbal cue *sit* and the hand signal. When all is said and done, you will find that the release word (*okay, all done* or whatever you choose) becomes the reward in and of itself for the behavior. Needless to say, it's important to issue a strong release each time.

DOWN

· · · · · · · ·

Now that you're well on your way to achieving a reliable *sit* from across the room by using only a simple hand signal, let's talk about *down*.

Once you, **not** Bozo, have the methods of teaching the *sit*, *down*, and *stand*, you can (and I think it's a very good idea to so do) ask for all three in some sequence. Then, especially for the super-energetic dog, you can ask for a *sit*, *down*, *stand*, *down*, *sit* in a repetitive sequence.

DOWN

Day 1

Have your fortified bag of kibble (a few liver treats added for excellent performance) at the ready. Let Bozo know it's "game on" by giving him a freebie piece of kibble.

Ask Bozo to *sit*. Hold the kibble between your thumb and index finger with your hand in a palm down position. Then, while he's in a *sit*, say "Bozo, *down*," and quickly move the piece of kibble in front of his nose, straight down to the floor between his front paws. Hold it there with your palm down. His attempt to get it should cause his body to slide backwards into a down. To facilitate this exercise, move the treat very slowly along the floor towards Bozo's chest. When his bum is on the floor and he's lying down, say "Yes," and treat. Repeat 3–5 times and that will do for this session. **Be patient**. Bozo may need time to figure it out. Remember though, no down, no reward!

Repeat 3–5 times throughout the day.

Day 2

Vary the task. Sometimes ask for a *sit*, sometimes a *sit* and then a *down*. Reward for the best/speediest performance only

Occasionally, as you're moving around your house (always armed with kibble, of course), ask Bozo for a *sit* using only a hand signal. Give him a liver treat for speedy compliance. This will maintain his interest. He never knows for sure what's coming next...but there MAY be a reward involved. We humans get this...it's like playing the slot machines!

Continue to ask for a *sit* and a *down* frequently as you move about in your day. This ensures that a Bozo will be asked to perform the required actions in many different locations...both inside and outside your home. You might want to use your parked car as a training tool as well. Have him *sit* before jumping in or out of the back seat (or before you pick him up if he's too small to jump). While Bozo is sitting in the back seat, you get to sit in the front seat, alternating from driver to passenger sides, each time asking for *sit* and *down*. You will want to do this, of course, while your car is stationary!

Not all puppies are food motivated. Thankfully, most are. If your Bozo is not, make sure:

1. that you schedule training sessions when he is hungry;

2. that the lure/reward is something especially tasty; and

3. if a squeaky toy or a good tug-of-war toy engages him better, use that but be sure to reserve this kind of activity for training lure and reward, at least for now.

For the *down* hand signal, extend your arm in front of you below shoulder height with your palm down and make a downward motion toward your thigh. As you introduce this, be sure to move your arm **first**, then say, "Bozo, *down*." Repeat and wait. If, after a few seconds, Bozo is not *down*, return to the luring stage, standing a step or two away from him this time. Use the same hand signal and command as you move your 'lure-holding' hand down between his forepaws.

When you have completed a session, (4 or 5 successful repetitions), be sure to praise Bozo and release him with your release word—*okay*, *all done*, or whatever you choose.

Now we have a *sit* to a *down*. Let's shake it up a little and do the reverse: a *down* back to a *sit*.

Okay...so Bozo is lying nicely in front of you. Waggle a treat in front of his nose, your palm facing up. Move the treat quickly up and back over Bozo's head. Up he comes. Or maybe not...if he has rolled over or is disinclined to get up, take a step backwards, pat or scratch the ground, or clap your hands. As he begins to move, step in quickly and lure him to a *sit*. Reward Bozo's first few successes, and then reward him only for speedy performance. Keep raising the bar!

Finally, ask for *sit, down, sit*...rewarding only after the final *sit.* Terry Ryan of Legacy Canine calls this a '3-fer' (three moves for 1 treat).

Every time you add a new request (command) to Bozo's repertoire, remember to ask for an older command as well...on its own and as part of a sequence. For example, now that you have *down,* ask for it anytime you see Bozo sitting.

Next time we'll add *stand* and then we'll glue all this in place with *stay.*

KNOW THIS:

It is important to have **ALL** members of the family involved in Bozo's training. Everyone needs to be on the same page, philosophically, regarding Bozo's training and everyone needs to use the exact same methods, commands and reward system.

If you're the "in charge" person, it's your job and responsibility to ensure that everyone does. This is absolutely critical for the continued development of a well-mannered and reliable family companion.

STORYTIME

. . . .

FREE TO ROAM

"Well, I'll be darned! That's Rosie," I thought as I automatically put my foot on the brake. "She doesn't venture onto the highway, huh?" That's what her owner had told me a few weeks before.

I love that dog... I admit to having a huge mushy spot for the Bully breeds. A huge, white, beautifully muscled American Bulldog, Rosie had appeared in the driveway of The Dog House several months before. In fact, she appeared there quite regularly. Sometimes we shooed her away. Sometimes Heidi drove her home. Her owner feels strongly that Rosie should be free to roam. We do not. That major philosophical difference is unlikely to be resolved anytime soon.

Right now though, Rosie is on the downside of the highway, which means she has crossed it once and the cars are whizzing by. I pulled in ahead of a white jeep parked on the narrow shoulder. The woman inside was on the phone—calling animal control? I don't know. I tapped on her window.

"Do you know this dog?"

"No."

"Well, I do. I'll get her and take her home."

"Need any help?"

"Nope. I'm okay, thanks."

Thankfully Rosie was more or less standing still behind the Jeep...her whip of a tail slashing the air as I approach.

"C'mon, girlfriend," I said as I hooked my fingers in her collar.

We waited for another spate of cars to pass and I took her to my car.

"In you go," I said, opening the car door.

Rosie hopped into the back seat and immediately set to enjoying the doggy smells... it's Jack's seat.

Whew! Crisis averted.

"You know, Rosie, that's the second time you and me and the highway have met. Not good. That's just not good. If I came upon you injured or worse, I'd..."

My mind drifted away into what I'd like to say and do to her owner... violent, unspeakable, socially unacceptable things. Her owner's dog owning philosophy, which is as outmoded as the horse and buggy, is endangering this beautiful sociable, agreeable creature on a daily basis.

"Home we go, Miss Rosie."

Eventually I found where she lives. Pounding on the door produced no results.

"OK, then, it's Cedar Creek for you," I said as we headed to the kennel that also acts as a holding facility for strays.

"Oh, Rosie. Yeah, she's been here before," says Sarah, the young attendant at the kennels as she prepares to come and relieve me of my passenger. "I have the phone number right here."

I was somewhat astonished to hear that this was Rosie's second or perhaps third visit to Cedar Creek, especially since each visit costs money—not enough, apparently, to be a deterrent! Rosie, completely unfazed at the prospect of being confined, enjoyed a cookie and a kiss with me before Sarah came for her.

"I'm glad you're safe for today," I thought as I drove away.

Isn't keeping them safe an integral part of loving our canine family members?

STAND

· · · · · · · ·

Muddy, wet Bozo comes in the door and *sits* like the well-trained puppy he is. If he knows how to *stand* when asked, the drying off becomes much easier for you and him. It's also a useful position for trips to the vet and the groomer. Of course you have kibble in your pocket. After all, there's kibble in the pocket of everything you own, isn't there? (At least for these first weeks!)

So, standing about a foot or less in front of Bozo, kibble (or treat) held between thumb and index finger with your sideways-turned palm facing him, waggle the kibble in front of his nose as you take a small step backwards. Move the kibble straight back towards you parallel to the floor. Say, "Bozo, *stand.*"

As Bozo moves to get up, lower the lure a little, still keeping it parallel to the floor. (If he continues to look up, most likely his bum will drop into a *sit* again.) Therefore, you may find it easier and more comfortable for you to teach many of these requests while you are kneeling on the floor, upper body upright, especially if Bozo is a wee lad.

As soon as Bozo is standing, say, "yes," and reward. Repeat 4–5 times. That's a session. Have several sessions on the day you introduce *stand* and in the last one, bring Bozo from a *down* to a *stand* and back to a *down*, using both a vocal command and a hand signal.

When teaching the *stand* from a *down* position, say, "Bozo, *stand*," then waggle the treat in front of his nose and move it straight up and back towards you (the same as from a *sit*). If he's comfy or settled in a *down*, scratch or tap the ground in front of you to get his attention or upgrade the reward to something of higher value—say, a liver treat. Praise and reward for speedy compliance.

To reverse...that is from a *stand* to a *down*, say, "Bozo, *down*," and quickly lower the hand holding the lure, palm down, in front of his nose to the floor, between his forepaws. Hold your hand still and wait for Bozo's elbows and chest to touch the floor—the play bow position. Once that happens, move the lure towards his chest. That ought to drop his hind end to the floor. Say "yes" and reward. Be sure to amp up the praise for this one. It's difficult.

Dr. Ian Dunbar gives an alternate method for teaching a *down* from a *stand.* Using either your leg, as you sit on the floor with one knee bent upwards creating a bridge, or a coffee table, say "Bozo, *down*," waggling the lure in front of him. As he sniffs it, move it away from him, either under your bent leg or under the coffee table. Bozo will lie down to crawl underneath and voila, *down* from a *stand*! Thanks, Ian. As always, do 4–5 repetitions to create a session. Repeat the session 4–5 times a day. At the end of each session, always remember to release.

There, now. Bozo pup knows *sit, down*, and *stand*, and he can change from one to the next. The next step is to sequence your requests...*sit-down-stand-down* or *down-sit-down-stand* or any other combination you choose.

Just remember to be patient, especially if Bozo is not a natural athlete. Give him time to comply.

STAY

. . . . . .

Good on you! You now have a puppy who will *sit*, *down*, and *stand* on request. Excellent!

You will find, though, that at many times you will want Bozo to *stay* in one of those positions. Let's add that now. Some say that *stay* is implied in the initial command (i.e. sit and stay there until I release you). I, personally, like the added clarity of *stay* so that both Bozo and I know exactly what's expected.

If your pup has a default position (for Jack, it was *down*), start with that. If not, choose *sit, down* or *stand* and begin there. *Sit* will likely be easier than *stand* as a starting point.

Standing in front of Bozo, say "Bozo, *sit*. Good boy. Bozo, *stay*." (I like the policeman's "Stop!"—hand raised, palm forward—as my hand signal for *stay*. It's quick, effective, and visible from a distance.)

Now, break eye contact with Bozo and turn your head away. If he stays, praise and reward. Move to another location. Repeat. Move again. Repeat. This time, move some part of your body—a foot or arm—that will indicate to Bozo you are going to move. If he *stays*, praise and release. You may want to use rewards occasionally as you teach something new. By now, though, the release should be the reward.

In the next session, always being sure that you have Bozo's full attention, ask for the *sit* and *stay* and then take a step away from him. So far, so good? In a low and quiet voice, tell Bozo what a good boy he is. Take another step away. Stop. Again, tell Bozo what a good *stay* this is and then enthusiastically release him ("*okay* or *all done*...good boy, Bozo!") If he moves before you release him, return to your position in front of him, ask for a *sit* and *stay*, wait 5 seconds, then praise and release him. Take it slow and easy, adding a couple of seconds to each request and moving only a step at a time in any direction while asking for a *stay*. Remember to vary locations for this exercise and stay very focused during the early stages so that you can release Bozo **before** he moves. We want to set him up for success, right?

When you have achieved a 3-minute *stay* and a distance of about 10 feet, increase either the time or distance a small amount at each repetition. What is YOUR goal? 5 minutes at 20 feet? You can get there! All it takes is a little time, patience, and persistence.

As you increase your distance from Bozo, be sure to move backward, while facing him. That will enable you to see if he's even thinking about moving. If you sense that he is, then immediately release him. It's always better to issue the release command **before** any movement happens.

Don't expect too much too fast. In other words, vary your expectations depending on each new location, duration, distance, and distractions...not to mention the size and breed of your dog. Mere seconds will be an achievement for a tiny breed at first. The larger more sedate breeds aren't so keen to change positions and will probably be content to *stay* more readily. Then there are the frisky, active breeds...do try and match your expectations to their personalities. You CAN teach them all. YOU need to be flexible in your expectations.

Once Bozo has demonstrated that he has grasped this concept (i.e. he *stays* when directed, ask him to stay in a *down, stand*, or *sit* several times throughout the day. Praise him for staying while he is staying. Release him when you're done. Reward Bozo only occasionally and/or for spectacular performance. If you have stashes of rewards in various rooms in your house, you will appear to Bozo to be a magician as you cross the room and return to him with a treat. It's a lottery; he just never knows when rewards will appear. That keeps him interested.

When initially released, Bozo may not move. That's okay. It's his choice. You just carry on. He just needs to figure out that *Okay* or *All done* means that the session is over and he's free.

The long distance *stay*, say from across a field or a road, is a wonderfully useful tool for you to have in your arsenal. If it is reliable, it can afford Bozo off-leash freedom (where permitted, of course) in situations that have the potential to be stressful or downright dangerous. Of course, you would never put Bozo or yourself, for that matter, in that sort of situation unless you knew with 100% certainty that you have a 100% reliable *stay*.

SETTLE

. . . .

Imagine, that upon hearing the words, "Bozo *settle*," your four-legged friend instantly lies down quietly. No more begging at the table, no more nudging you, no more yanking his leash when you stop to visit a neighbor while on a walk.

It's important to interrupt play sessions with Bozo... especially when he's very young. Uninterrupted play sessions quickly deteriorate into an out-of-control free-for-all. Not good for pups—worse for humans. So, from the beginning, stop the play sessions every 30 seconds or so for a couple of seconds only, then release him. Use *leave it* to have Bozo release the toy or tug-of-war object and as he grasps (no pun intended) that concept, ask him to *settle* just for a second or two. After 30 seconds or so, have him *settle* again for an additional 2 or 3 seconds.

Frequent repetitions of "Bozo...*settle*," followed shortly thereafter (a few seconds will do) by, *okay* or *all done* (or your own release word...it matters not what you choose) will increase the pace of his learning.

Your TV watching time offers another excellent opportunity to teach Bozo how to *settle.* Put him on his leash, or position him on his mat or in his crate somewhere near you. Calmly ask him to *settle*. When he does, reward him with a peanut-butter-smeared chew toy—any stuffable chewtoy will do. (I really like cylindrical ridged rubber ones for this lesson.) During the commercial breaks (they're perfectly timed to last 2-3 minutes), release Bozo for an active play session and then have him *settle* again when the program resumes. As always, it's best to work up gradually to long *settles*, so you'll want to start with brief 'time-outs' in the course of longer play periods.

KNOW THIS:

Dogs do what works for them.

If *settle* is followed by play, or *settle* means a tasty chew toy will soon follow, or *settle* means a walk resumes, Bozo won't be long figuring out how this process can work very much to his advantage. You'll be amazed.

I don't believe you can over-praise your dog so be sure to give Bozo lots of affectionate encouragement for all the things he does when you ask. Quick caution, though... if Bozo is in a *sit, down*, or *settle* position, or if your voice is particularly high-pitched, be sure to keep your tone and volume level closely monitored when praising him. Higher-pitched voices (typically women's and children's) are great motivators, which is very useful when seeking activity (*Come* or *Let's go! or Go get it!*) but need to be notched down a few pegs for non-active requests.

If, like me, you like to stop from time to time while out on a walk...to sit on a park bench and enjoy the outdoors or read a paper...having Bozo know how to *settle* will mean that you can sit for a while and he'll be happy to do the same...especially if you produce a stuffed chewtoy. (I strongly suggest, however, that something other than peanut butter be used when going walkies. I tend to find that peanut butter can be so messy in your pocket!) Be creative!!

Strategy:

- Introduce frequent, brief interruptions into your playtime with Bozo (*settle;* praise; release).

- More play. Increased *settle* time.

- Change locations

Sure, you can say, "Bozo, go to your mat." But think about how many more places you can use *settle*.

SPEAK & SHUSH

Dogs bark.

It's not bad...and hardly abnormal. It's what they do. In fact, barking is likely one of the main reasons that man, thousands of years ago, kept dogs close and chose to domesticate them rather than run them off. But I do get it. You know that the barking is normal but it's driving you nuts, right? It can and probably will if you don't learn how to control it.

> KNOW THIS:
>
> Dog training is nothing more than taking a dog's natural behavior, be it barking, walking, sitting, digging, chewing, or fighting and putting it *on cue*: in other words, making Bozo do any of his normal behaviors when **YOU** ask for them.

Pretty simple concept, huh? But teaching Bozo the cues takes time, practice, and patience. It's so worth it!

Back to the barking.

Here's one for you...first you have to get Bozo barking.

"Excuse me?"

That's right. You do.

Enlist the help of a friend, neighbor, or family member and have them stand outside the door while you and Bozo stay inside...just behind the closed door. Say *speak* or *woof* or *bark*. That's your accomplice's clue to ring the bell or knock loudly. When Bozo barks, praise him. Repeat several times, changing doors, if that's a possibility in your home. It won't take long before Bozo hears the doorbell or knocking and barks, as if on cue. That's it! You've taught him *when* to bark.

Shush or *quiet*.

Okay, so Bozo is barking.

With a treat at the ready, keeping very still, stand close to him. Say *shush* or *quiet* or *enough* (just one word) and waggle the treat in front of his nose. He will stop barking to check out the treat. Praise and reward. Then, ask Bozo to *speak*. When he does, quietly ask for *shush* (treat ready) after 2 or 3 woofs. Repeat 3-5 times (that's a session). Repeat the session 3 or 4 times a day.

If you have permitted Bozo's barking to escalate and become its own motivation, which should definitely be avoided, you will need a high-value reward to stop it simply on your *shush*. Barking should be stopped after only a few 'woofs.' After all, we want to set Bozo up for success. For example, if you've only had a couple of days practice with *speak* and *shush* and you're in a far part of the house when he starts barking at a passerby or a squirrel or whatever usually sets him off, you can try calling out *shush* **once**. If he stops, excellent. Be sure to praise him lavishly. I think it more likely, at this stage he will not stop...but if he doesn't, do NOT keep yelling *shush.* Either get yourself to him and distract him with a treat, a toy, or a favorite activity or ignore him until you have successfully taught him the *speak/shush* sequence. To this point, you've taught Bozo to relate the *speak/ shush* request to a knocking door or ringing doorbell. Don't expect him to generalize that particular instance of *speak/shush* to all situations. Dogs don't usually generalize well. Instead of getting upset that Bozo is now barking at the mailman, the kids next door, etc., utilize these opportunities to teach more instances of *speak/shush.* The key to success is for you to recognize what triggers the barking in the first place. Is it the kid whizzing by on a skateboard, the garbage truck, a cat crossing the yard?

Maybe you want him to bark at the garbage truck... especially if you have a habit of forgetting to put the garbage out. What about the cat in your yard? Maybe Bozo should be allowed to tell you about that, not because he's not fond of cats, but wouldn't you rather a cat chose its own yard as a litter box? For sure, there are times when you want Bozo to bark. What you don't want is a frenzied,barking maniac...out of control barking for no apparent reason, especially when he's home alone. You **CAN** teach Bozo when it's okay for him to bark...you just need to agree on when and how much (5-6 woofs is usually sufficient). You (and your neighbors!) will be happy if you do.

STORYTIME

. . . .

TILLEY

"Is that an Irish Setter pup?" I asked, watching this beautiful red pup playing with the 'big kids.'

Months before we bought The Dog House, I visited the previous owners simply to enjoy being surrounded by a pack of dogs. There were maybe ten or twelve dogs here that day, all playing in the front yard. One was obviously a pup and her red color led me to believe she was an Irish Setter.

"No, no," I was told. That's Tilley. She's a cinnamon Golden." It didn't take Tilley long to undulate her way over to me and insinuate herself between the others who had gathered around. Leaning against me, she slid onto the deck, tipped her head back to what seemed like neck-breaking point, and checked me out. Then she was off.

By the time we moved in, Tilley was a young adult. By then, she had perfected her early ability to push through the horde in order to be close to her chosen human and she never failed to lovingly greet all our guests.

Tilley's most endearing quality is her immediate acceptance of all dogs. Big, small, old, young, quiet, playful… she didn't discriminate and was always able to be with them all. If we had 'players' in-house (those who love to run and run and run), Tilley was up for that game. If there was a new dog who was a little reserved at first, Tilley did her magic and made the newbie feel welcome. When we had a prospective dog client coming for the required one hour 'interview', we knew it was far more likely to go well if Tilley happened to be here that day. Tilley, in fact, was so reliable in dealing with the other dogs that appointed her our Social Director.

Tilley turned 5 in February 2011 and she's been coming here for nearly all of those five years. Interestingly, her 'come all ye' personality has become somewhat more discriminating during that time. She has definite ideas now about whom she'll play with and who should have the ball. She and her best buddy, our Charley, frequently vie for possession. It works best when Charley wins. He brings it back. Tilley does not.

Still charming and friendly to visiting dogs, Tilley's ability to insert herself into any group to be close to a visiting human is now an art form!

Our Tilley-Wit-Boom (where the heck did that come from?)…we love her!

COME...THE RECALL

I have heard it said, "If your dog doesn't *come*, you don't have a dog." Not quite sure that's so, but instead of debating it, let's teach your puppy to *come* whenever and wherever you ask.

It's all part of the manners game—*sit* for leash on, *sit* for leash off, *sit* before going through a doorway, *sit* for dinner. All these required *sits* keep Bozo's energy under control. If Bozo's energy is controllable, he's biddable.

My observation has been that dogs don't come when called because they're having too good a time doing doggy things. They have experienced that responding to "Come!" simply means the end of the fun. We've all seen and perhaps even played, the catch-me-if-you-can game in which Bozo makes up all the rules, the owner gets increasingly loud and frustrated, resulting in shouting and lunging and eventual capture of 'wild dog.' Not a fun picture and totally unnecessary.

Come needs to be taught, just as you have taught all the other requests, in a variety of locations. Starting indoors in a small space, when Bozo is 3-4 feet form you, squat down, open your arms wide and say, "Bozo, *come.*" When he does (and do make yourself interesting enough that he will!), give him a big hug and lots of praise and then release him with, "*Okay*, *all done,* or *go play.*" Interrupt your own activities several times throughout the day and repeat this exercise. Make the distance a little greater as Bozo's understanding increases and offer an occasional reward for an especially prompt performance. It's the 'slot machine' thinking again...if you reward every recall, Bozo won't get the idea that speed is important. It's the element of uncertainty that keeps him on his toes. Make sense?

If you have a fenced yard and can enlist a volunteer to assist you, move the exercise outdoors. Starting with a short distance between you—say six feet or so—have your assistant hold Bozo as you back away holding a reward. With your arms outstretched, say, "Bozo, *come,*" and come he will, usually at a great rate of speed. Small dogs sometimes can't find their brakes and run right past you. Larger pups can take you down. When Bozo is a couple of feet from you, ask for a *sit.* When he slides into a *sit,* give him a big hug and lots of praise. Now, have your assistant call him. Same routine as before. As you continue to play, increase the distance between you and your assistant and reward Bozo for particularly speedy performance and /or *sit* upon his arrival. Again, five repetitions are plenty for one session. At the beginning of your next session, later in the day or even the next day, start with one recall at a shorter distance (review) and then make the distances increasingly longer. It is ideal if you have a set-up where the person calling Bozo is out of sight (e.g. around the corner of the house or behind a shrub).

Now is a great time to play with Bozo for a few minutes—throw the ball, have a tug-of-war, roll around on the floor/ground. Whatever works!

As Bozo's skill at *coming* improves, add distractions in the yard—kids going by, a person passing by with something of interest to Bozo in his/her hands. Ignore them and continue with the exercise. If Bozo ignores them too, that's fabulous...and is certainly deserving of a treat! If he doesn't, walk away a short distance for a few seconds. Then, start again with "Bozo, *come*."

Now it's time to add another dog to the mix. Invite one of Bozo's doggy friends and his owner to join you. Interrupt the play session frequently with a, "Bozo, *come*." Do **NOT** repeat louder and louder. That's "blah, blah, blah" to Bozo, and likely more annoying, the louder it gets. It won't help.

If Bozo seems to have lost his memory with the appearance of this new and exciting canine distraction, ask your human visitor to hold on to his dog for a moment. Ask Bozo for a short distance *come* several times. If those are successful, on the last one while Bozo is sitting beside you, give your visitor the nod and release Bozo with a "*Go play!*" Very soon after play resumes, say, "Bozo, *come*." Either he does and then gets to 'go play' again or the visitors disappear. He'll get it. Be patient. **Do not repeat continuously, "Bozo, *come*."**

Until Bozo has a solid *come* with the dog distraction present, he's not ready to be tested in the dog park. Work with him (and limited, controllable distractions) until he's 100% distraction proof (well, close to 100%, anyway). It is excellence we're seeking; not perfection.

You can see from the *go play* that playing with his canine friends is a much higher value reward for Bozo than kibble or a liver treat. Thus it becomes a give and take experience. "Bozo, if you do as I ask, I'll let you do what you want to do." This is true of everything you teach him. **IF** he complies with your request, the reward is something he wants to do.

So, pay attention... I'm talking to YOU! Whatever it is that Bozo is indicating he wants to do, use that activity as the reward when he responds positively to your request.

"Bozo, *come*. Good boy. *Go play*."

LEASH WALKING

. . . .

Without a doubt, the easiest way to have your puppy walk calmly **on** leash is to play *follow me* **off** leash. How do I do that, you ask? Read on.

Move away from Bozo and keep moving. (It is not possible to follow a stationary object.) If he doesn't follow fast enough, move faster. If his attention gets diverted, clap your hands, say something like, "Come along!" and move quickly in another direction. If he rushes ahead of you, turn around and move quickly back the way you came. Your constant moving away from him keeps Bozo focused. Encourage him as he follows you. If he can't depend on you to stay still, he'll soon figure out that he needs to keep an eye on you at all times.

You can start this in his long-term confinement area when Bozo is very young... as soon as you get him home, in fact. After he's pottied outside, you can play *follow me* in the kitchen, living room, anywhere, really...and the more places, the better. Obstacles work too...around the table, behind a chair. And don't forget outside. If your yard is fenced, that's a great place. Both you and Bozo can move quickly and cover longer distances.

If Bozo lags or stops, clap your hands, and move away from him. If you decide to shorten the distance between you by moving towards him (to make it easier for the little fella) it won't be long before Bozo is leading and you're following him. That will not be helpful when he's on a leash.

Once Bozo is 3 months old, find somewhere safe that you can walk long distances. Stop lots and ask him to *sit* or if a large sitting rock lures you, bring along a stuffed chewtoy and ask him to *settle*. If he roams off, run in the opposite direction. Hiding behind a tree will keep him attentive too. Don't take YOUR eyes off HIM. Call out his name from behind the tree. (You'll have noticed we haven't been using his name to keep him following you. If you're hiding, though, it seems only fair!) Offer lots of praise as he comes bounding towards you. Kids are particularly good at this. They move quickly and that keeps Bozo on his toes. Do supervise. The *follow me* (**he** follows **you**) is important.

Some independent breeds may be more easily distracted. Does this mean they can't be taught to walk on a leash? Not at all. Redouble YOUR efforts. Make yourself more interesting than the distraction. Talk to a squeaky toy, zigzag quickly, make a noise like a cat...be creative. Never forget: puppy training is FUN!

DO NOT DELAY IN STARTING THIS EXERCISE.

An adolescent dog (5 -6 months) is far more interested in doggy things than he is in you. If you start early and continue this training, by the time Bozo reaches adolescence, you'll have a Velcro dog! (Though 'elasticized Velcro' might be more what we're looking for.) Then, just snap on the leash and off you go. That simple? Yes...with a few cautionary words.

Allow time for the introduction of the leash. Ask Bozo to *sit* before attaching the leash and wait for him to do so. It may take a few minutes of bouncing and bobbing about. If you stand still, he will *sit.*

Praise him and snap on his leash. Most likely that will cause him to rocket to the end of his leash. Stop. Stand still **until** he *sits*. Praise him. Then say, "Let's go!" and take one giant step. You may only be AT the door at this point. That's okay. Remember to ask for a *sit* before you open the door.

Once you are outside, continue to take one giant step, stop, ask for *sit,* say, "Let's go!" and take another step, same as before.

Once Bozo *sits* immediately when you stop, try taking two steps before stopping. Those two steps must have a slack leash—like the letter "J" between you. Gradually increase the number of strides you take, three, then four, then five before stopping and it won't be long before Bozo *sits* as soon as you stop. He has learned that his *sit* makes you go again. Pretty smart, huh? Now you can go for a real walk.

You're moving along nicely and suddenly the leash goes taut. Bozo has spotted something of doggy interest. **STOP**. I repeat, **STOP**. This is where pulling begins and either you deal with it **right now**, or become the human Bozo walks for the rest of his life. Or, worse still, there are no walks because Bozo is a 'puller.' There is a simple three-step solution to this common problem...though it's not necessarily an easy one. The training here is for YOU, not Bozo. Ready?

1. The second the leash goes taut, STOP.

2. Turn and walk in the opposite direction for a few steps.

3. Stop and ask for a *sit* before resuming the walk

4. Say, "Let's go." Start walking

It is of critical importance that these steps be followed **every** time the leash goes taut. The steps are easy, as I'm sure you'll agree. The tough part for us is being consistent.

KNOW THIS:

Behavior you reward is reinforced. Praise or treat or resume activity for correct responses. IGNORE unwanted responses.

The first time you ignore the taut leash, you telegraph to Bozo that pulling is okay.

When I got Jack, I knew how to stop the pulling. What I didn't get, though, was what I was telling him by not **ALWAYS** stopping. By age 10, he'd slowed down to the point where people had stopped asking me, "Who's taking whom for a walk?" All that pulling that could have been stopped if I'd had the self-discipline to consistently enforce the primary rule of a puppy on leash.

Notice how there are no (or very few) treats/rewards involved here? That's because the activity (the walk) is the reward. Bozo understands that. Do you?

ROLLOVER

. . . .

"Bozo, *roll over*."

"But I don't need or want to teach my dog party tricks," you say.

Fair enough but consider another view. *Roll over*, apart from the oohs and ahhs it will evoke from your audience, is an incredibly useful tool whenever you, the vet, or the groomer has reason to examine Bozo's undercarriage. "Bozo, *roll over*," in fact, makes it incredibly simple.

Convinced yet? Good. We'll carry on then.

Have Bozo in a *down-stay*. Give him the initial 'game on' piece of kibble. With another piece of kibble in your hand, move your hand back along the side of his muzzle (towards his body) and over the top of his shoulder blades. The pup will begin to roll. Keep moving the lure until he has rolled all the way to his other side. Praise profusely and give him the kibble. Now, say, "Bozo, roll the other way." Keep moving the kibble over his shoulder blades again until he has rolled back to his original position. Praise and treat.

Hint: If Bozo is not inclined to roll over on your first attempt at this exercise, tickle him ever so gently in the groin area. That ought to make him raise one hind leg and you're on your way.

You can also start this exercise while Bozo is lying on his side, instead of in sphinx position. Once you've lured him to his back, you can ask for a *stay* in that position as well by holding the lure treat still. You may want to name this posture (on his back, feet in the air) something like, 'dead dog.' It then becomes something else that Bozo does naturally that you have put on cue (i.e. taught him to do when asked).

To get a *roll over* from a *sit* or a *stand,* ask for a *down* using the palm down, hand moving downward signal, followed by the hand moving in an arc over the shoulder blades once he's in the *down.*

As you already know, repetition is the key to learning. Be mindful though not to do so many repetitions that you stress Bozo. So, do the usual 3 -5 reps, and call it good. Don't forget to release him. *Sit, down, stand, come,* and *roll over* are now all cues that Bozo understands. It is important to continue to ask for each and every one of them in different locations regularly and often (that's reinforcement), as you go about your daily routine.

Has Bozo now learned to do something new? Well... yes and no. He could always roll over and lie on his back. What he has now learned is to do it upon request. If you make the cue (command) for the dead dog position, "Bang!" the kids will love it and I bet you'll have no trouble getting that one repeated frequently!

If you go for the "Bang!"—dead dog, I can guarantee some very entertaining moments when you do this especially if you ask for it while on you're on a walk.

Have fun!

HEELING ON AND OFF LEASH

You may think that teaching your dog to walk in the *heel* position (on your left side with his nose parallel to your knee) is only useful or necessary for those who participate in obedience trials. Not so. *Heeling* as a practical application for anyone who has ever had to navigate busy streets or crowds of people. In addition to that, teaching your pup to *heel* is good mental stimulation for both of you. In puppy hood, Bozo is a veritable sponge: learning comes so easily. Why not take advantage of this golden opportunity? You know, my constant, 'more, sooner, is better.'

I don't remember if I've used the phrase, "Be a splitter, not a lumper," for you yet (thank you, Terry Ryan, of Legacy Canine). To simplify teaching Bozo to *heel,* splitting the lesson into very small steps will make it easier for him and far less frustrating for you.

To begin... actually, **before** you begin, be sure Bozo's *sit* is solid and reliable. Now, with a lure (ball, Frisbee, food treat) in your left hand, direct Bozo into a *sit* on your left side. Now, you take one step in any direction. Stop. Say, "Bozo, *heel,*" and lure him into the *sit* by your left side. Repeat this one step exercise many times and in many different locations both inside and outside the house. With lures in both hands, begin to pivot in place, always having Bozo finish by *sitting* beside you on your left. Mix it up. Pivot right, pivot left, pivot 180 degrees.

Provide constant positive reinforcement as Bozo moves. Make the distances short. This exercise requires a lot of concentration on your part; you will probably need to refocus many times. If it all falls apart, breathe deeply, reposition Bozo in a *sit* on your left side and begin again.

KNOW THIS:

Puppy (dog) training is not so much about the puppy. It's about teaching the humans to stay focused, committed and disciplined.

OK, so where are we?

Bozo sits on your left, you step out, and say "Bozo, *heel*," he complies and moves to a *sit* in the new position. You've turned in all directions, always using the correct starting and finishing position and kept your attention on Bozo as he moves to each new position. Excellent! Now you're ready to begin gradually increasing the number of steps you take: two steps for several sessions, then three, then four and so on. Remember, if, when you add a step, you lose Bozo, go back to the previously successful number. Have patience. It will happen.

Move quickly, just as you did in *follow me.* Keep the distance short and the line you're walking straight, at least at this stage. Provide lots of enthusiastic encouragement and praise (and the occasional treat!) to your clever pup and a pat on the back for yourself too. This is complicated stuff and it's about to get more complicated.

Up until now, every sequence has been *sit, heel, sit*—which meant if you wanted to change directions, you did so with Bozo in a left side *sit* and then you stepped out in the new direction. Now we want Bozo to make the right or left turn while he's still moving.

Turning right:

Walk more quickly. Move your left hand out in front of Bozo's nose (with or without a lure/reward...you know your puppy by now). When his head is ahead of your left knee, turn quickly to the right and continue walking for a couple of steps, praising Bozo when he returns to *heel* position. Then, stop, *sit*, and repeat. If you move with speed and intention through this step then there's no time for Bozo to make other plans.

Turning left:

Slow down a little. Move your left hand back past your left knee. You may want to say "easy" or "steady" as you do to give Bozo the cue. Make the turn and praise Bozo when he returns to *heel* position. Walk a few steps, *sit,* and repeat. 3-5 repetitions are enough...but you should plan to have several sessions throughout the day.

Heeling is big stuff for Bozo to learn so be sure to give him some extra time and attention when the session is over. Walking Bozo off your property will be much more pleasurable for both of you if he knows how to *heel* before you snap on the leash.

As you set off down the street, remember to stop often and ask Bozo to *sit*. Vary your speed to keep him attentive and remember to give him lots of positive feedback. There are lots and lots of smells for Bozo out there in the big world and it's hardly fair to keep him in the *heel* position for an entire walk. Do alternate *heel* with free ranging. Use your release word to let Bozo know it's okay to smell the flowers and then ask him to *heel* again when you want to move along at a faster pace.

It is said that dogs regard 'walkies' as the #1 treat in the world. Quite frankly, when I have a dog beside me, I agree.

STORYTIME

* * * * * * * * * * * * *

Miss Ella

Gus was waiting for her when she stepped off Rainbow Bridge. He greeted her, canine fashion, with a good sniff. "Welcome, Ella. Good to see you. You'll find lots of friends here—Meggie, Bud, Antonio, Molly, Chelsa, Wren, Jamieson, Penny, Gordy and Bart." The two former Dog House buddies gamboled away to find the others, pain and disability forgotten now.

Ella, when she lived on this planet, was an Airedale. She was a regular, though infrequent, visitor to The Dog House. Our whole family, canine and human, was fond of her and her human, Tricia. Ella had her own particular take on Airedale ears which would never have passed Airedale 'standard' but which gave her a distinctively 'Ella' look. Add rimless spectacles and, voila...the absent-minded professor.

In one hip she had a metal plate, the result of being hit by a car in her younger years. Her mobility was not impaired other than jumping up, which she never seemed inclined to do anyway. That said, we all felt that sitting outside on frosty grass was not good for her plated joint. She disagreed. We called, cajoled, lured...all to no avail. Ella turned her head away in disdain and made her own decisions as to when she'd come inside.

Ella's dignified demeanor barely disguised the mischievous delight contained in her black and tan wire-haired body. As we would head out on a morning trek to the lower field, she trembled impatiently at the gate, ready to explode with the others in the open space beyond. I smile when I think of her, as I was always aware of her sense of delight and humor about the world around her.

Until very recently, Ella loved to join the pack for the daily field trek when they all tore around like canines possessed! The field for her, though, was more an opportunity to freshen her favorite fragrance (*Eau de Sheep Poop*) than anything else. When there were horses down in the field, Ella, on orders from her mother, was denied access. No amount of bathing removes the pungent odor of horse manure! It's all subjective, really. I don't think dogs are necessarily appreciative of our choices of perfume either.

"Woo, woo, woo," was Ella's way of adding her opinion to any conversation. Amazingly, by simply changing the tone slightly, she was also able to request a head rub. When Ella got excited, humans stand firm! She didn't hesitate to come between legs (and with no regard whatsoever as to the length of said legs). Each of us experienced that uplifting experience at one time or another. It never failed to evoke a laugh.

Jaunty, joyful Ella....gone at age 8, like Gus, far too soon. We, who loved her, are grateful for the many wonderful memories of 'Ella the Belle.'

BITING

· · · · · · · ·

Truthfully, my knowledge about bites and their severity is limited. There is excellent information available and I will give you a couple of sources after I share a few of my thoughts.

Really and truly we don't teach Bozo **how** to do anything. What we teach him is **when** it's OK for him to do what comes naturally. Did we teach him to bite? No, that comes built in. What we **did** teach him was to inhibit his bite on humans. Does he still bite and chew on his toys? Most certainly.

If you've ever watched a genuine dog fight, you'll remember that the noise was intense and probably your immediate thought was, "One of them is going to be killed." That is rarely the case. Am I recommending you let a dog fight continue to its natural conclusion? Not at all, if you can *safely* intervene. Repair bills at the vet are expensive.

We have experienced the sharpness of Bozo's teeth, that's why we taught him to inhibit his bite before his jaws developed sufficient force to inflict real damage. Later in life, if a well-inhibited bite has been established and Bozo becomes frightened or injured and he snaps or bites, it is unlikely he'll cause any real harm. "Real harm." That's really what we really want to avoid, isn't it? Even in extremely hurtful circumstances, we want those teeth to stop short of breaking skin. Let's not kid ourselves. A dog has the strength, force, and speed of bite to kill a human. That said, it's very rare that they do.

Dr. Ian Dunbar, to whom I refer frequently, came up with a standardized way to evaluate bites. I'll reprint it here with the kind permission of Terry Ryan from whose book, *Coaching People to Train Their Dogs*, I have taken it.

BITE EVALUATION SCALE

LEVEL ONE

Air snap. This is a warning bite that doesn't connect. The dog intentionally inhibits his bite and 'missed' on purpose. The dog is doing everything possible to get your attention and tell you that all is not well. There were probably many signs leading up to this snap.

LEVEL TWO

Air snap with skin contact. There might be a red mark or a slight bruise, but the skin is not punctured. The dog has purposely not bitten down hard. The dog is inhibited to bite, but could be losing that inhibition. If Level One and Two snaps are not working for him, he could escalate to Level Three.

LEVEL THREE

There may be one to four puncture holes from a single bite. Skin punctures are no deeper than **HALF** the length of the dog's **CANINE** teeth.

LEVEL FOUR

One to four holes from a single bite, deeper than half
the length of the teeth. There is soft tissue damage
such as (a) severe bruising telling us the dog clamped
down HARD; and/or (b) slashes in both directions
from the puncture indicating the dog bit and shook
his head.

LEVEL FIVE

Multiple Level Four bites with deep punctures or
slashing due to clamping down, shaking, or repeated
gripping in an attempt to move the bite to a 'better'
advantage.

LEVEL SIX

The victim dies as a result of the attack.

Dr. Dunbar summarizes that 99% of all dog bites are
Levels One through Three, and mostly Ones or Twos.

In her book *Dogs Bite, but Balloons and Slippers
are More Dangerous*, Janis Bradley provides data and
graphs to illustrate her point that many things are more
dangerous than dogs and their bites. I recommend it.

No one is saying that a biting dog is acceptable in our
society. Perhaps a greater understanding of Ian Dunbar's
'bite levels' and the relative rarity of harmful dog bites
would go some distance in alleviating the paranoia that
permeates society today, especially regarding certain
breeds.

THE FOOD BOWL AND OTHER POSSESSIONS

. . . .

Resource Guarding

"Grrr...Grrr...don't touch my food!"

Oh my, what happens to the agreeable puppy of mere moments ago when his food bowl is placed on the floor? Apparently he doesn't quite get that humans don't want his food...and he surely can be quick to warn us to keep away. This behavior, like so any other anti-social and unacceptable behaviors is 100% preventable. The answer, of course, lies in teaching your very young pup how you want him to behave. Surely, growling at the one who feeds him is **NOT** it!

Using his daily ration of kibble as training and behavior molding rewards means that Bozo is likely more accustomed to feeding from your hand than a bowl. If that's what you've been doing, good on ya! Some days, however, at the end of the day, you'll find that there is kibble left from his daily ration. Would you like to put it in his food bowl? Okay...but let's set Bozo up for success right from the start.

It goes without saying, of course, you will ask Bozo to *sit* before putting his meal down. I'm sure you're familiar with the old adage—"leave the dog alone while he's eating"—but I'm going to suggest the exact opposite. By all means, leave an adult dog to eat alone in peace if you wish. We're talking about a puppy here and eating alone serves neither him nor you. Stay with him.

KNOW THIS:

Eating alone fosters protectiveness, not sociability.

So here's what you're going to do: get a couple of pieces of chicken, cheese, or some other tasty tidbit, sit on the floor beside Bozo and while he's eating, put a 'surprise' in his dish. Your stock immediately goes up as the magician who makes treats appear! On another occasion, take his bowl away mid-meal and add a spoonful of canned food. Wow! Having a human around at mealtimes is great! Be sure to include all family members in this. Friends, too, if they're willing.

This next idea comes from Dr. Ian Dunbar in his book *After You Get Your Puppy.* He calls it 'the delinquent waiter routine.' I love it.

Put Bozo's empty dish down on the floor. He'll check it out. "Hmmm, no dinner. What's up?" Pick up the dish. Put one or two pieces of kibble in it. Put it down. As soon as that's gone, do it again. You can even add a few seconds' delay before adding the next few bits. You'll have Bozo's attention, for sure and he makes the positive association between you and his food.

As I mentioned, this is all dead easy when Bozo is very young. If you have been tardy in starting this exercise, and

Bozo growls or lunges when you reach for his bowl and you back off and don't know what to do next, get help from a professional trainer immediately. Otherwise, it will only get worse.

Can you see the connection between taking away and giving back the food bowl and taking away and giving back toys? If the thing goes away and never comes back, you create reluctance in Bozo to give it up in the first place and suspicion when you attempt to take it...or even come near.

Teaching *take it* and *leave it* (or *off*) with kibble or toys, assures Bozo that when a thing goes away, better things show up—praise and reward—and eventually, so does the thing he gave up. That builds his confidence and trust in you. I think that's important. Wouldn't you agree?

VETS AND OTHER HEALING MODALITIES

I have heard it said that vets are the most respected professionals in the world. I have great respect for their knowledge and dedication. I respect my own physician, as well, but I wouldn't dream of handing over responsibility for my health to her. I like to do my own research, form my own opinions and then work in tandem with my health professional. I feel the same way about my pets' health care.

There's a long list if everyday issues that may arise with Bozo: diet, fleas, worms, vaccinations, digestive upsets, to name a few. If it is your decision to simply place the decision for treatment into your vet's hands, that's fine. It's **your** decision and for a variety of reasons you may not feel competent or confident in dealing with even the everyday issues yourself. If, however, you are knowledge-driven or merely curious, I suggest you talk to dog owners in your area...ask lots of questions and seek references for various canine health practitioners. Then do an Internet search for things like the pros and cons of vaccinations, when to spay or neuter, blood titers, how diet can deter internal parasites, how to deal with fleas...the list goes on. Check out several sites—not every site says the same thing—and then apply your own common sense to what you've read and proceed from there.

If you are fortunate enough to have a holistic vet who is reachable by phone, as I am, call him/her and seek advice, too. Just to be clear—a holistic vet is one who looks at the whole picture of the animal rather than just the physiological perspective.

Merriam-Webster defines holistic as relating to or concerned with wholes or complete systems rather than with the analysis of, treatment of, or dissection into parts. Because you know your puppy/dog, his daily activities, his normal energy level, his diet, his personality, a holistic vet will want your input on those things, as well as any physiological issues in order to diagnose and treat any problems.

Many years ago, someone gave me a homeopathic remedy to counteract Jack's negative reaction to a vaccine he'd had. At the time I knew nothing, and I mean nothing, about homeopathy. With good luck, reasonably good judgment, and the information available to me, I had... and continue to have...great success using homeopathic remedies on my dogs—and myself too! Veterinary homeopathic practitioners are easier to find now than they once were and their knowledge can be helpful. Check it out.

Believing, as I do, that canine energy (unlike human energy) is untainted and clear, it's no surprise to me that dogs respond well to energy work and therapies. Both my dog, Jack, and I have enjoyed real benefits from Reiki, for example. I've also seen Charley, another of our dogs, respond well with less-stressed and calmer behavior after Reiki. Consider also, healing touch and Tellington Touch. Do your homework. See if any of them may be beneficial now or in the future. Animal chiropractic therapy is also available now...and if you've ever had an adjustment yourself, you can perhaps imagine how good Bozo can feel. An adjustment is particularly useful after a hard play dislocation or a 'sports' injury. Acupuncture, too, is a viable alternative and warrants checking into.

As the human responsible for your pet's health, decisions regarding his care are yours to make. We are fortunate to live in a time when so much knowledge is available to everyone. That's not to say that everything you read, or are told, is to be swallowed whole as the truth. Never suspend your own judgment. However, as a friend of mine once said, "Knowledge is a light load to carry around."

Enjoy the search.

FUN & GAMES

. . . .

It's all fun and games, isn't it? I mean, really, isn't learning easier when you're having fun? Every time you play with your dog, there's an opportunity to teach him something new or to reinforce something he already knows. Play, I believe, is essential to the bonding process and bonding is essential to the training process...besides, if there's no bond between you, why do you have a dog?

"Bozo, *fetch*; Bozo, *drop it*." Whether it's a ball or a Frisbee, I'm betting you'll tire long before he does!

When you're starting with a little fella, you'll want the distance you throw (more likely, toss) any object to be short. You can ramp up Bozo's interest in the object by fussing it up or talking to it before you toss it. Have him *sit* or *stand* or *stay* while you toss it (once he's learned these things of course!). In the early stages you may need to be prepared to 'trade' in order to get the thrown object back. Great! Really, you're just having fun: the opportunities to teach or reinforce are right there.

Some dogs are adept at catching. You'll quickly find out is your Bozo is one of those dogs. If he is, catch can become part of your ball game. In the winter, catching snowballs is great entertainment!

Tug-of-war is always a winner. I have heard people discourage it on the basis it may make the dog aggressive. Not so, I say, as long as you have lots of rules—**YOUR** rules established **BEFORE** you start. This applies to all games with Bozo. With tug-of-war, a couple of things to bear in mind are:

1. Stop the game frequently with *drop it*, *give* or whatever your *give it* word is. Resume after a brief pause; and

2. His teeth should never touch your skin. Even if it's accidental and doesn't hurt, say "ouch" in a very offended tone and walk away for a minute or two. Then you can resume.

With kids, a great recall game is **hide and seek**. This only requires you (or another adult) and one child. If there are more, so much the better! Send the kid(s) off to hide, armed with a treat. You restrain Bozo (if necessary—he doesn't have a solid *sit/stay* yet). Have the child call out "Bozo, *come*." Let Bozo go find the child and be rewarded with the treat. If the child is old enough, tell him/her to have Bozo *sit* before he gets the treat. (It's important that you have already shown the child how to offer a treat and that he/she is comfortable doing it.) Young children have a tendency to choose the same hiding place over and over. Encourage and help them to choose lots of different spots. This is a great indoor rainy day game.

So is, **Go to...** if you have more than one child. Either you or one of the children has Bozo *sit* beside them. While standing very still, he/she says "Bozo, *go to* Jim."

Immediately, Jim, standing across the room, kneels down, opens his arms wide and says, "Bozo, *come*." When Bozo gets to Jim, have Bozo *sit*. Praise and reward him. Then Jim says, "Bozo, *go to* Peter," and back to Peter Bozo goes. In the first few 'gos,' Bozo can have a treat for compliance. After that, no treat, just praise. Sometimes, Jim or Peter will have to do something to make himself interesting. As Bozo gets better, add distractions—maybe play outdoors in a safe place. The reward and release for this one can be *go play*.

Kids love the **dead dog pose**. If you decide to teach Bozo to *roll over*, by using a gun finger hand signal and the verbal cue *bang*, kids will be more than happy to help you reinforce that one.

Consider **Freeze tag** if you have a group of kids. You will need to have taught Bozo to *freeze* beforehand. Like the word *wait*, it has many uses. As always, be sure to make up the rules ahead of time, interrupt the game frequently for brief moments, and **supervise**. Kids, like dogs, can quickly get very wound up.

Depending on your chosen breed and your inclination, you can teach Bozo to *sit up* (front paws in the air), *shake* (give one paw), *high five* (similar to *shake*), *dance* (standing on hind legs, paws on you—or freestanding if he's built that way—and moving to music) or balance a biscuit on his nose.

Carl, a bouncy yellow Lab who often comes to The Dog House, astonished us all with his motionless, squarely placed *sit* while he balanced a biscuit on his nose, then cleverly caught and ate it on the *okay* signal. Taking into account the build and personality of your puppy, you really can teach him anything his body construction will allow. Take your cues from things he does naturally, on his own. Then put it on cue.

If Bozo is not quite ready or old enough for agility class, perhaps you'd consider setting one up in your own back yard. Weave poles, a jump, and a teeter-totter are all easy enough to construct. Do an Internet search and insert 'agility' into the search field. You'll be amazed at what you find.

Hidden treasure works best outside (and in a designated area) but you can play it inside using the couch, chair his crate, pillows, etc.

Swimming, woodsy off-leash dog walks (**solid recall is an absolute must**!), soccer, city on-leash walks...all these can be fun for you and Bozo. In fact, most things, especially walks, are way more fun with a dog!

STORYTIME

. . . .

ZACH'S BUCCANEER[4]

"Just one?"

How could we choose just one of the eleven brand-new yellow Lab puppies? But choose we did, Zack's Buccaneer—Buck or Bucky Boy for short.

While he grew and learned with his littermates and his mom, Honey, we visited and after what seemed like a very long time, we were able to take Buck, or Mom Puppy, as I affectionately called him, to his new home—our home.

Buck's new world was an exciting place...the great outdoors lay before him to explore with his dad, Zack, and his kids, Kate and Sam(antha). Rest time found him asleep on the kitchen floor, his head practically under the burning woodstove. Each time he got up and moved, I was always surprised not to find a puddle of brains lying where his head had been.

Bedding, pillows and his doggy bed were comfortable enough for Buck but paled in comparison to the comfort

---

4 Contributed by Lisa Beenen, the author's daughter.

of the bottom bunk in the girls' bedroom. Was it the mere comfort of the bed that was so attractive to him or was it deliciously enhanced by its being 'off-limits?' Hmmm.

Buck's brother, Hoover, belonged to my sister who visited frequently. When the two boys were together, tearing around the house and racing through the garden were favourite games...and 'who's got the rubber boot?' provided endless entertainment for dogs and humans alike. A peanut butter stuffed Kong® was amicably (sometimes, at least) and frequently shared.

And then there were the chickens. I think the chickens dreaded to see them coming. No day would be complete without Buck and Hoover noisily checking on the chickens' activities. "Too bad about that fence," Buck would say to Hoover every time.

The first winter was the best. First came the never-before-seen white stuff. Then, under the watchful eye of Daddy Zack, the boys discovered turnips frozen into the ground. Needless to say, digging them up was a great game and the delightful frozen turnip snack that went to the victor was seriously enjoyed.

When summer came, Buck made an exciting new discovery—moles! He stalked them and he caught them. Buck, the hunter! That lovable, pleasant face had us all fooled for a while but kissing Buck came to an abrupt halt once we realized the wildlife that had crossed his lips!

Buck was a good dog.

He missed his dad when Zack crossed over Rainbow Bridge. Rex, his new companion, a former neighbour and nemesis, now shared his home and together they spent several more years exploring the woods at Triple Creek Acres until the family moved to town.

I think Buck's favourite human was Kate. She spent lots of time brushing him, playing with him and dressing him up. He loved every minute of the attention. I'm sure he had many thoughts of, "Kate's the best!"

All in all, we had a happy and well-spent 15+ years together. We miss you, Buck, but we are so grateful you picked us to be your family. You were the model of a perfect family dog. We're glad that you are now free of pain and happily roaming the far side of Rainbow Bridge with Zack, Gus and all your new friends.

CHOOSING A PUPPY CLASS

. . . .

"But I've potty trained Bozo, taught him to *sit, down,* and *come* AND I've had people over to meet him. Now you want me to take him to class?"

That's right. I do. If indeed, you have done all those things, good on ya! That said, everything that you have done thus far has been done in isolation because Bozo's immunization protection was insufficient to expose him to other dogs and public places. Now that he's three months old, his immunity is building nicely and unless he's one of the slower-to-mature large breeds, adolescence with all its uncertainties and insecurities, is fast approaching.

With other things besides his immunity to consider, beginning puppy classes when Bozo is 3½-4 months old offers a reasonably safe, clean environment where he can catch-up on his dog-to-dog socialization. Granted, a people-loving, dog-fearful dog is easier to live with than the reverse, but why not have a totally well-adjusted and socialized puppy who meets all people, dogs, and situations calmly and with enthusiasm and confidence?

Needle sharp teeth and sensitive skin create a zero
tolerance attitude towards a too-hard bite. The bitten pup
will yelp his displeasure, mid-play and it's game over...at
least for a few seconds. Be sure to watch. Their timing is
exquisite.

How will you find the kind of puppy class you're
looking for? And while we're at it, what kind of puppy
class should you be looking for? The first one is easy. This
is the information age! Do an internet search of your area
using 'puppy classes' in the search field. That will, at least,
let you know what is available and where. Personally, I
would prefer to see an online video clip...the information
highway is great for that, too! Failing that, word-of-
mouth is usually a safe bet. Once you've narrowed your
search, you're halfway there. As for what type of class
you're looking for (or moreover, want to avoid), I'd start by
making a few phone calls. Ask questions...get a feeling for
the facility, the instructor(s), and the methods employed.
Among the first words I'd want to hear in any answer to a
query about methods would be: reward-based, off-leash,
and playtime. If there is no mention of choke collars,
metal collars, and/or physical punishment, **ASK**. Those
methods are a throwback to the Dark Age of dog training

and are, fortunately, not so prevalent today. Sadly, they do still exist.

If there are several classes in your area that sound promising, ask if you can come and observe before deciding. Leave Bozo at home. This will give you even more of a sense of what you are getting Bozo into. If an instruction facility is not willing to let you come and audit a session or two, it's probably best to cut your losses and move on. They're not our kind of people. Period.

My personal preference would be a family-oriented class where all family members get to participate by taking turns working with the puppy and where there is plenty of off-leash playtime with lots of brief interruptions for instructions and settling.

A 50-minute to 1-hour puppy class ought **not** to be a lecture, in my opinion. Apart from the puppy's short attention span, the human on the other end of the leash will have great difficulty staying focused or interested in a stream of instructions and information from the instructor. Puppy classes are about 'doing.'

Above all else, puppy classes ought to be FUN... fun for the puppies, fun for the owners, and fun for the instructor, too. While this step of puppy socialization is serious and important, there's no reason at all not to have a good time. We don't learn any better or faster by being earnest and serious about it—quite the contrary.

So go...interact with other puppy owners (keeping one eye on Bozo at all times), be attentive to the instructor, observe the puppy interaction, and above all... HAVE FUN!

ARE WE DONE YET?

* *

The big world beckons. Are you and Bozo ready?

His immunity is building, his people socialization is excellent, and his dog-to-dog socialization is up to par now that he's in puppy class. Your wee, wiggly, sweet-smelling puppy is growing up! Doghood is just over the bridge of adolescence.

Just as with humans, adolescence is a time of heightened interest in one's own kind...a time to focus on what it is to be a dog...a time when exposure to new people and things can create uncertainty. Be warned, adolescence is the time when everything you have spent these last 8-10 weeks teaching Bozo can go flying out the window with alarming speed.

As all of us mothers know, we despair of our young children ever voluntarily offering "please" and "thank you" until that one magical day when we finally hear it and the one million repetitions become instantly worthwhile. Other than an occasional reminder, we congratulate ourselves that we've successfully taught that lesson. Inexplicably, as the teen years arrive, "please" and "thank you" mysteriously depart. But we know that gentle and, if necessary, **constant**, reminders will cement "please" and "thank you" permanently into place.

Voila! Polite adults. It's similar with Bozo. *Sit, stay, come, settle*, and *shush* are manners which you have already begun to firmly instill in him. Throughout his lifetime, though, they will all need to be kindly and consistently reinforced...particularly through his adolescence, when the adventure and excitement of elevated hormones can block out all else. Although Bozo's retrieving and scent discrimination skills may develop with your leadership, I hope his number one, all-time favorite hobby is (or becomes!) chewing on stuffed chew toys. Oh, the expense and despair you'll save yourself if you get his chewing habit well established early.

KNOW THIS:

Adolescence is **NOT** the time to just 'let Bozo be' in the dog park, playing with his canine buddies. Continue to interrupt his play sessions with a *come, sit*...and then praise and release to *go play*.

Continue to invite new people to meet him. New dogs, too. If you make a daily walk with Bozo one of your life's little pleasures, you can continue to meet new people and new dogs. Why not drive to another part of town for your walk? Both of you can enjoy and be energized by the change of scenery. I planned to go for a walk early this morning—by myself, as Jack's walks are more slow strolls now—only to be met by torrents of rain. As I removed my jacket, deterred by the rain, I thought, "If I had a dog who expected a walk, rain would never stop me...snow wouldn't either, for that matter." I think that going for a walk with a dog—either on or off leash—is one of life's greatest pleasures. Teaching Bozo how to walk nicely on a loose leash, to *heel*, to *come* when called when he's off-leash, and a reliable *sit* at a distance will ensure many, many pleasurable outings.

Bozo *sits* to greet visitors to your house now. He will *settle* on request while you enjoy a meal or a good book. Of course, he barks when someone comes to the door but *shushes* when asked. You have used this window of opportunity (8-16 weeks) well and you now have a puppy whose basic manners are in place...who likes people of all ages, meets new dogs with confidence, and who has a reliably inhibited bite. It has taken much time, patience, and consistency of effort on your part. There is a bumper sticker that says:"A dog is a lifetime commitment ." I agree. In fact, my becoming a puppy trainer was strongly influenced by my desire to help new owners teach their new canine companions the behaviors that will keep a puppy in its FIRST home FOREVER.

So...no, you're not done yet... . In fact, you won't ever be DONE but with the groundwork in place, constant and consistent reinforcement through adolescence and beyond, you and Bozo can expect to enjoy many years of companionship and fun together.

Well done, YOU!

STORYTIME

. . . .

HAPPY BIRTHDAY, JACK

My 68th birthday looms large on the horizon...the 'young old,' I think it's called in today's parlance.

I'm blessed with good health and a sound mind. Even so, I can't now move as quickly as I used to. I've lost some flexibility and balance and arthritis calls out to me from several joints. I'm just NOT 29 anymore! Thankfully, I haven't yet reached the stage where I get confused, am unsteady on my feet, or need help with routine activities.

Jack has though.

Today, May 21st, 2011 Jack celebrates his 13th birthday. Given his breed, Bulldog/Boxer cross (Valley Bull), I figure he's been 'living on borrowed time' since he turned 10. Despite chronic renal insufficiency (failing kidneys), an enlarged prostate, and arthritic shoulders, elbows, hips and knees, he gets along on a fine day when he has a mind to. Unlike me, Jack does need some assistance with routine activities. As much as he loves a car ride, he can no longer jump out when we arrive at the park (he can't depend on his shoulders) so I lift him gently to the ground. He waits for it. He can manage to get into the car by himself, ever so slowly, but I stand by with empty hands in case he slips. He would find that embarrassing.

On cool or rainy days—we have lots of those here on the Coast—Jack shows no interest in a stroll...what used to be a fast-paced trot. Instead, he snores contently on the heated back seat of the car while I run errands. During a recent cold, wet spell, even though he was wearing his dashing red fleece-lined waterproof coat, he refused to leave the garage.

"Not for me," he seemed to say as he turned back toward the kitchen door. Entirely his call. I no longer insist upon his doing anything he doesn't want to do—well, take his meds, perhaps, but that's another story!

I figure Jack has earned the right to do as he chooses and my role now is that of his facilitator! Gone are the days of tug-of-war with Gus or me; gone are the days of leaping off the ground behind the ball-thrower to snatch the ball on the backhand. No longer does Jack nudge me to get up at first light. In fact, he sleeps at least two hours later than I do. He still expects the two treats that signify my departure without him but he doesn't catch the second one anymore. Either he can't be bothered, or he simply can't do it. Who knows?

"Jack, the Recycling Dog" was his former title, earned because he never passed a discarded plastic pop or water bottle that he didn't dutifully carry home with him, no matter how far. His younger brother Gus pretended not to notice that Jack was carrying anything until we crossed the threshold of 'home.'

"Mine," Gus then said. "Mine," and dashed off with his prize. His job done, Jack paid not the slightest attention.

If we're still using 'times 7' to convert human years to dog years, Jack is 91 today. Wow! When I'm 91 and slow to move and think, and I make less active choices, I hope that those who assist me will have the requisite patience and compassion that dear old Jack has taught me.

Happy Birthday, Mom's Boy!

APPENDICES

. . . .

COMMON TRAINING MISTAKES

- Lack of a clear plan. It is critical to have a plan (i.e. what to do when Bozo jumps up) and ensuring that **everyone**, including visitors, follows it. Stay with it.

- Impatience. For Bozo, English is a second language and must be learned. Imagine someone saying, "Duduk!" to you. Would you know it meant *sit?* Of course not. (Unless you're Indonesian.)

- Use of force. You'll get compliance but you'll lose trust and respect. Is that what you want in a family companion?

- Yelling. As with kids, yelling raises the level of negative energy and causes confusion.

- Sessions that are too long. Puppies have a short attention span. Use short (3-5 minutes) sessions repeated many times throughout the day

- Rewarding inappropriate behaviors. If you don't like the behavior, ignore it. That will stop it (Patience. Remember?). Shushing or yelling will only provide the attention Bozo seeks.

- Timing. Reward the wanted behavior at exactly the moment it occurs. Stay focused.

- No puppy training. Regardless of the size of your puppy, he needs to be taught manners in order to be a well-behaved adult.

- Discontinuing training too soon, or ever, for that matter. Training and reinforcement is a lifetime affair. It never stops.

- Continuing to use food rewards. Phasing out the food rewards is essential to reliable responses.

- Starting late. You can train a dog at any age but why not take advantage of its early training window? So much easier and infinitely faster.

- Insufficient reinforcement in the early stages of training. You're teaching a lot of things all at once. Keep those rewards coming—intermittently and at random—to be sure, but DO keep them coming.

BLUE POWER EAR TREATMENT

A knowledgeable young dog lover in a health food Store gave this to me many years ago. Both Gus and I were at the end of our respective tethers as his nighttime head shaking kept both of us awake! It worked like a charm!

This formula has been handed down from a wonderful veterinarian, now deceased. Many have also found it effective for cuts, fungus between toes, and small tumor-like cysts, but it must be faithfully prepared and **applied as instructed**. I would remind you that ears are very sensitive and your dog may appreciate having it warmed up a bit. I've found the best way to warm up the solution is to place it in a cup or glass of warm water for half an hour or so.

Ingredients[5]

16oz. Isopropyl Alcohol

4T Boric Acid Powder

16 drops Gentian Violet Solution (1%)

Mix all ingredients together in the alcohol bottle and shake well. (You will also need to shake the solution every time you use it to disperse the Boric Acid Powder.) To use, purchase home haircolour-type plastic bottle to dispense solution to affected ears.

---

[5] I usually make half this amount and I mix it right in the dispensing bottle

Method

Evaluate condition of the ears before treating. If they are very inflamed and sore, do not attempt to pull hair or clean out. Wait until inflammation has subsided (about 2 days). Shake Ear Treatment Solution well before each use. Flood the ear and massage gently to the count of 60. Wipe with a tissue. Flood again with solution, wipe with tissue, no massage. The dog will shake out any excess solution, which can be wiped with a tissue. Warning: Gentian Violet does stain fabrics (and white dogs!)

Treatment Schedule

Treat twice per day for first week to two weeks, depending on severity of ears

Treat once per day for next one to two weeks

Treat once per month (or less frequently, depending on dog)

All of these ingredients should be available at your local pharmacy. Despite the alcohol, the dog will not object even to the first treatment. The Boric Acid Powder soothes the ears. The Gentian Violet solution is an anti-infection agent.

The solution appears to work on any and all ear problems from mites to earwax to canker. After the second or third day you can clean out the ear with a Q-tip or cotton ball. The success rate for this treatment is 95-99%.

Those who do not succeed have usually not done the treatment long enough or have not been regular about it. Dogs on the verge of ear canal surgery have been returned to normal with only the follow-up treatment to keep the ear healthy. If an infection seems to be remaining in the treated ear after the above course of treatment, the ear may have some pseudomonas bacteria in the site. This can be eradicated by using a gentle flush of raw apple cider vinegar and warm water. Use two tablespoons of vinegar to one cup of water, twice per week.

© 1998

LIVER TREATS...GOOD & CHEAP

Liver.

I wonder what pictures that word conjures up for you? Yummy liver, bacon & onions or yucky liver that you had to eat because "it's good for you?"

Yummy, yummy, yummy—that's a dog's opinion of liver...especially in the form of treats. Tiny pieces of freeze-fried liver treat make a high value training reward, which you can also crumble, over a bowl of kibble to inspire even the most finicky eater.

Liver treats are super easy to make and cheap, too. If you choose organic liver, it will be more expensive, but surely a healthier choice. Here at 'the hacienda' we've recently raised lambs, turkeys, and roaster chickens. None of the humans were excited at the prospect of liver, kidney, or heart (my kids still tell the story of *disgusting* Hawaiian Chicken Livers that I served and *they* ate), so I took the batch of organ meat, sliced it thin, put it on a foil-covered baking sheet and baked it in a 250° F oven for 4-5 hours. Voila, dog treats!

I store them in a covered jar in the fridge. You've never seen as many attentive dogs as those who appear in the kitchen when I begin to unscrew the lid of that jar!

There you have it...cheap, easy, high-value treats!

A couple of tips:

You can parboil the liver (and other organ meats) first. It's easier to slice that way. I never bother. Boiling them creates another pot to wash!

If you forget to cover the baking sheet with foil, plan to throw it out!

RECOMMENDED READING

Dogs Bite: But Balloons and Slippers Are More Dangerous *by Janis Bradley* ©2005 James & Kenneth Publishers, Berkeley,California

Why We Love The Dogs We Do:Finding The Dog That Matches Your Personality *by Stanley Coren* ©1998 Fireside (a trademark of Simon & Schuster,Inc.), New York, NY

The Culture Clash *by Jean Donaldson,* ©1996, 2005 James & Kenneth Publishers, Berkeley, California

Dr. Dunbar's GOOD LITTLE DOG BOOK *by Ian Dunbar* ©2003 James & Kenneth Publishers, Berkeley, California

The Other End Of The Leash Why We Do What We Do Around Dogs *by Patricia B. McConnell, Ph.D.* ©2002 A Ballantine Book, The Random House Publishing Group, New York, NY

The Puppy Primer *by Patricia B. McConnell, Ph.D and Brenda Scidmore* ©2010 McConnell Publishing,Ltd., Black Earth, WI

On Talking Terms With Dogs: Calming Signals *by Turid Rugaas* ©1997, 2006 Dogwise Publishing, Wenatchee, WA

Made in the USA
Charleston, SC
26 May 2012